That's What . . .

I'm Talking About

(Collected Essays & Reviews)

Richard Baldwin Cook

That's What I'm Talking About
(Collected Essays & Reviews)

Second Edition 2008

Copyright Richard Baldwin Cook

ISBN-13: 978-0-9791257-0-6
ISBN-10: 0-9791257-0-7

Nativabooks.com

Nativa LLC
Cockeysville, MD

Other books by Richard Baldwin Cook:

**MAY IT PLEA$E THE COURT
ALL OF THE ABOVE I
ALL OF THE ABOVE II**

Available at On Line booksellers & Bookstores

All Drawings by Leah Fanning Mebane
www.fanningart.com

TABLE OF CONTENTS

CONTENTS	i
ACKNOWLEDGEMENTS	3
INTRODUCTION	7
HUNGRY PEOPLE	13
FARM WORKERS – FROM THE SHADOWS INTO THE LIGHT	19
THE FIRST AMENDMENT	45
MAL CAMINO MAL DESTINO	51
PAUL & HIS VICTIMS	53
PAUL . . . PREACHER OR EVANGELIST ?	93
PAUL THE ORGANIZER	99
ST. PAUL: PREACHER / ORGANIZER	121
PAUL TAKES A FIRST AT CAMBRIDGE	131
"I CANNOT LISTEN TO THIS ANYMORE"	141
THAT WHICH YOU HAVE BN GIVEN	143
SHALL THE DEAD RULE THE LIVING?	145
PASS BOLDLY INTO THAT OTHER WORLD	147
(BUT TO . . .) KNOW THE MIND OF GOD	149
A SPIRITUAL BAKED POTATO	153
QUAINT BUT CREDIBLE	155

DISCERNMENT, NOT DOCTRINE	159
A SHRILL ARGUMENT, THEN BLOOD	163
A DICHOTOMY THAT WON'T DI	165
APOSTOLIC SPHINX	171
YOU WANT ME TO CUT OFF . . . WHAT?	179
"SHOULD I GET TO HEAVEN . . ."	185
INDEX	215

ACKNOWLEDGEMENTS

Permission to reprint is gratefully acknowledged.

Articles:

"Hungry People Want to Feed Themselves (Not be Fed by Others)" *Seeds* (Sept 1979), pages 8-9

"Paul ... Preacher or Evangelist," 32 *The Bible Translator* No 4 (October 1981) pages 441-444

"Paul, the Organizer," Vol IV *Missiology* No 4 (October, 1981) pages 485-498

"St Paul - Preacher, Evangelist or Organizer?" Vol 93 *The Expository Times* No 6 (March 1982) pages 171-173

"Farm Workers: From the Shadows Into the Light," Vol 2 *Faith and Mission* No 1 (Fall 1984) pp. 40-55

"The First Amendment and Religion," *Pulpit Digest* (July/August, 1988), pages 62-65

"Paul and the Victims of His Persecution: The Opponents in Galatia" 32 *Biblical Theology Bulletin* No 4 (Winter 2002) pages 182-191

"Paul Takes a First at Cambridge," 34 *Biblical Theology Bulletin* No 2 (Summer 2004), pp 87-90

Reviews:

Berlin Diaries, 1940-1945 by Marie Vassilchikov, titled here, "I cannot listen to this anymore" *Pulpit Digest,* Nov/Dec 1988, pages 47-48

Roger's Version by John Updike, titled here, "That which you have been given . . ." *Pulpit Digest*, May/June 1988, page 48

Ironweed by William Kennedy, titled here, "Shall the Dead Rule the Living?" *Pulpit Digest,* July/August, 1988, page 46

The Dead, by James Joyce, titled here, "Pass Boldly into that Other World" *Pulpit Digest,* Sept/Oct 1988, page 51

A Brief History of Time, by Stephen Hawking, titled here, "(But to . . .) Know the Mind of God" (1989) *Pulpit Digest,* Jan/Feb 1989: page 46

The Counterlife, by Philip Roth, titled here, "A Spiritual Baked Potato?" *Pulpit Digest*, Mar/April 1989, page 81

Toyohiko Kagawa: Apostle of Love and Social Justice, by Robert Schildgen, titled here, "Quaint But Credible." *Pulpit Digest*, Sept/Oct 1989, pages 79-80

The Rain in the Trees, by W. S. Merwin, titled here, "Discernment . . . Not Doctrine" *Pulpit Digest,* Jan/Feb 1990, pages 81-82

Battle Cry of Freedom: The Civil War Era, by James M. McPherson, titled here, "A *Shrill Argument, then Blood" Pulpit Digest,* Sept/Oct 1990, pages 82-83

Paul Beyond the Judaism / Hellenism Divide, Troels Engberg-Pedersen, editor, titled here, "A Dichotomy that Won't Di" 33 *Biblical Theology Bulletin* No 4 (Winter 2003) pages 169-171

The Galatians Debate: Contemporary Issues in Rhetorical and Historical Interpretation, by Nanos, Mark D, editor, titled here, "Apostolic Sphinx" 33 *Biblical Theology Bulletin* No 3 (Fall 2003) pages 119-20

Cutting Too Close for Comfort: Paul's Letter to the Galatians in its Anatolian Cultic Context by Susan M. Elliott, entitled here, "You Want Me to Cut off . . . What?" 59 *Union Seminary Quarterly Review* Nos 3-4, 2005, "New Testament and Roman Empire"

"Should I get to Heaven," a sketch of the writer's great grandfather, taken from **All of the Above II** (2008), available together with **All of the Above I**

Excerpts from the poetry of Sor Juana: **A Sor Juana Anthology**, Alan S Trueblood, translator (Harvard University Press, 1988, pp. 40, 102), my own translations here. Pages 140, 158, below.

The poetry of Walt Whitman has been reproduced from his own 1891-92 compilation, published as **Leaves of Grass** (New York: Airmont Publishing Co, 1965, pp. 22, 28, 164, 226, 292-3, 342, 358) plus one poem from the posthumous collection of 1897, and published in **I Hear America Singing** (London: Anvil Press Poetry, Ltd 2001, p. 92.) See below, pages 6, 12, 18, 52, 162, 178.

Excerpts from **Fields of Courage**, by Susan Samuels Drake (Santa Cruz CA: Many Names Press, 1999, pp. 27, 67, 92-4). See Page 148, below.

Richard Baldwin Cook is a graduate of Union Theological Seminary in New York City and of Loyola Law School, New Orleans. He was a member of the staff of the National Farm Worker Ministry and, briefly, an attorney.

ONE THOUGHT EVER AT THE FORE

One Thought Ever at the Fore —

That in the Divine Ship the World, breasting time and Space,

All Peoples of the globe together sail. Sail the same voyage

Are bound to the same destination.

Walt Whitman

Old Age Echoes (1897)
Leaves of Grass

INTRODUCTION

We live in a swirling biosphere of connected fragments and forces. The trick is to catch the patterns. For some, coherence comes by way of revealed truth. For others, truth revealed does not exit. There are only facts that you get your mind around by awareness and work. But facts may or may not form a lucid pattern. By arranging facts yourself, you have not found a pattern; you have created an ideology.

My efforts to untangle the perception problem have been modified over the years, away from certitude and towards a greater appreciation of poetry and of metaphor. I have been helped by Walt Whitman to see the metaphorical principle. Whitman, THE poet of America, figured out that the historian is limited to life that 'has exhibited itself" while a poet, working through metaphor, can reveal life that "has seldom exhibited itself." (*"To a Historian," Inscriptions,* **Leaves of Grass**, 1891-92). I announce (hoping Whitman would approve): the Trinitarian guides to the vital patterns: work, awareness, imagination.

A theme which ties together these previously published pieces is reflection on the consequence in specific settings of belief in God. One believes in God by exercising one's individual capacities of mind. But then what? What does one then *do*? At earlier points in human history, a more communal and less individual orientation to matters of faith might have been the decisive element; but the communal components of belief inherently focus on ritual and not upon personal convictions.

Over the past five hundred years, in much of the world, individual choice in important, private matters properly has received the endorsement of civil societies. This trend has coincided with the development of representative government. The emphasis upon the private exercise of individual convictions limits the role of communal entities who would impose their doctrines. Enforcement is limited to those who choose to participate in the rituals. Even among participants there will be diversity of personal opinions about proper public policies and the actions of government.

In civil society, there is a bright line between sanctions imposed by communal entities upon their communicants and the employment of the coercive power of government, directed against non-communicants.

Why must this line not be crossed? The mechanics of Belief are not only individual; they are non-rational. The leap from a standing start to the stars is made on faith, if it is made at all. But civil society must operate upon a rational foundation. Policies must be approved, applied, and tested with resort to reasons and outcomes, which may be examined by anyone. The young Lincoln figured this out. In 1837, at age 29, he said, "Passion has helped us but can do so no more. It will in future, be our enemy. Reason - cold, calculating reason – must furnish all the materials for our future support and defense."

It is often the Religious who tend to try to cross the line between personal belief and civil policy and invoke coercive state powers in the interests of privately held convictions. There are good grounds for restraint. In the private setting, one who is "religious" may live out the revealed preconditions of eternity. But the "truth" embraced wholeheartedly in the personal realm, must remain privatized in the realm of civil conduct. The paradox of being alive and yet mortal ought to keep us from claiming, promising or insisting too much.

The paradox begins with consciousness itself. To be conscious that one is conscious, to be conscious that one's conscious self inhabits finite and failing flesh . . . the awareness of the brackets in which we live should elevate humility to the highest tier of values. Restraining our principled selves in our relations with other beings is one of the greatest challenges. Restraint is an urgent matter in a world in which a few individuals can do violence on a scale formerly limited to the actions of the State.

Our perception of ourselves as temporarily alive, of others, and of the cosmos within and around us engenders not only humility; this information also prompts a question: what to do? This question becomes an inquiry with a moral component (*how* to behave decently?) and an ethical component (*why* behave decently?). Both aspects often have been poisoned by the insistent demands of ethnic preferences and coercive religious exclusivism. These fraudulent values are a bequest of the ancient and then the medieval worlds, which were as suspicious of individual aspirations as they were of representative government.

There is a common ground upon which both rational and religious sensibilities may be reconciled. That ground is respect for the other. Respect incorporates taking responsibility in the civil realm, for the plight of those who are on the margins. Marginalized persons have civil claims, which require recognition and remediation because dignity and hope are preferable by every measure to brutishness and chaos.

Listening is a powerful stratagem. Victims merit a hearing; their own prescriptions are likely the best options; their preferences for themselves are likely to be what any similarly situated person would prescribe.

An example of respect deserved but absent from the civil realm is the one-sided struggle of farm laborers in the United States to organize so as to resist the vast, hostile powers which exploit them. A past example of disdain in the public realm is race slavery as practiced in the United States for 250 years. This condition formally ended generations ago by way of a bloody civil war, but the consequences and the legacy of race slavery resonate down the decades. We are not yet done with this horrific inheritance.

An ominous, present day expression of civil disdain, which appears to be taking fixed form, is the mistreatment in the US of Muslims, whether citizens, residents, or visitors. These persons appear to be poised just now to become victims of official and quasi-official campaigns of hatred and abuse. Since the three mass homicides of September 11, 2001, representatives of the government have developed the unsavory practice of asking an alarmed public to engage in a counter productive attempt to make endless war on *terror*, a noun, and *terrorism*, a tactic. The official announcements are couched in harsh and irrational ethnic overtones. This approach does not reflect Lincoln's appeal to "unimpassioned reason."

Before victims can be protected they must first be seen and heard. This dynamic in civil society involves a process of identification of both the victim and the abuser. Too often the civil process is aborted. The contemporary career of Agusto Pinochet – official terrorist - and the ancient career of the Apostle Paul - sectarian terrorist - have shown that a claim of impunity can extinguish, in every practical sense, the truthful accusations of victims.

Take Paul: the earliest believers in Messiah Jesus ("Jesus Christ") were Jews; they became the victims of persecutions conducted by Saul-Paul. His victims did not go quietly. They fought him. The survivors denounced him to his mostly Gentile converts, as his own letters attest. His victims attempted to undermine Paul's prestige and effectiveness as he promoted himself as a leader of the sect he had tried to wipe out.

For all this, Paul's reputation has not suffered. Why not? He changed his name and also changed the subject. The denunciations of people he abused and hurt were characterized by Paul as dangerous, mistaken theological positions; he framed their accusations as a disagreement about "the law" (Torah, mostly) versus faith in/of Messiah Jesus.

Paul claimed impunity for his own past conduct by asserting he was no longer subject to the old "law." Along the way, he reinterpreted Jewish Scripture and tradition in a breath-taking co-optation, which was so successful it is seldom recognized as the distortion it was - and is.

Victims of abuse and torture always are an embarrassment to the humanity of the bystander. Paul's converts, who were asked to take sides, probably wanted most of all for the victims just to go away. As a result, Paul's own statements, some turgid, some sublime, were preserved, then given canonical authority, and, for centuries, have been applied to circumstances unknown to him. While Paul has gone on to a sainthood of cosmic proportions, the victims who survived his persecution, together with their bitter accusations against him, have been received into the utter quiet reserved for the nameless and voiceless of history.

A few revisions have been made in these previously published pieces, mainly to smooth out some grammatical or syntactical flourish. No doubt, other bumps and blips have been added.

A SONG OF THE ROLLING EARTH

Each man to himself and each woman to herself,

is the word of the past and present,

and the true word of immortality;

No one can acquire for another – not one

No one can grow for another – not one.

Walt Whitman

Calamus
Leaves of Grass

HUNGRY PEOPLE WANT TO FEED THEMSELVES - NOT BE FED BY OTHERS

Creation itself will be set free from its enslavement to Corruption and receive the splendid freedom of the children of God. (Romans 8:21)

My first encounter with migrant farm workers was in the vegetable growing areas of New Jersey in 1970. Each summer thousands of migrant laborers arrive from Florida and Puerto Rico seeking work topping onions, picking tomatoes or cutting asparagus. Often an entire family would arrive from Florida and look for housing in a labor camp. Frequently there was no housing available, and when it was, it was often unfit for human occupancy. My work at that time (as director of a local Migrant Ministry) was to attempt to find temporary housing for individuals and families who literally had no place to live and little or no food or money. I became haunted by the terrible irony of working people in such conditions - people who harvest the food for the wealthiest nation on earth and yet are not able to have a house for themselves or food for their children.

Under the best of circumstances, it isn't easy to find a place to live. And for penniless farm workers in rural America, decent housing is almost impossible to find. My efforts to locate emergency housing were largely a failure. Communities that are happy to have the labor of farm workers are not at all happy to have the workers themselves. I came to ask myself: Wouldn't it be better if farm workers had control over their own lives and were not dependent upon the accidental presence of a "migrant ministry?" Wouldn't it be better if farm workers could house themselves? Wouldn't it be better if farm workers could take care of their own children? Wouldn't, it be better if the children themselves did not have to labor in the fields for the family to have enough to eat?

Yes. It would be better if farm workers had the resources to do these things for themselves - just as it is better for everyone to do such things for ourselves. But as soon as one answers "yes" to the liberation question one needs to ask a further question: *What is my responsibility to those who harvest the food that I eat?* The answer to this question takes shape in a series of propositions.

(1) FOR THE SAKE OF THE LIBERATING GOSPEL OF JESUS CHRIST, CHRISTIANS OUGHT TO ASSIST FARM WORKERS IN THEIR STRUGGLE TO TAKE RESPONSIBILITY FOR THEIR OWN LIVES.

Paul the Apostle wrote (Romans 8) that creation itself has fallen into corruption. Paul is speaking of the whole of creation and therefore the corruption is pervasive, including questions of personal morality, relations between persons, mortality, political and economic systems. But the final word spoken over God's creation is the word "freedom." For the whole of creation "will obtain the splendid freedom (liberation) of God's children." (Romans 8:21) This indivisible gospel of liberation surely extends to men and women who are struggling to effect a measure of liberation from an oppressive and corrupt economic system. (All economic systems are corrupted to a greater or lesser degree. What is required of Christians is, first of all, to *identify* those being oppressed and then *identify with* them.)

(2) THE FIRST STEP FOR THE MIDDLE CLASS CHRISTIAN TO TAKE IN THE DIRECTION OF FARM WORKER LIBERATION: LISTEN TO WHAT FARM WORKERS THEMSELVES ARE SAYING ABOUT THEIR CONDITIONS.

For almost 20 years [written in 1979] farm workers have been building their own organization, setting their own agenda, seeking collective bargaining through the

United Farm Workers Union, AFL-CIO. Cesar Chavez and those farm workers with him are making the life-long sacrifices which are necessary to bring lasting change in conditions for farm laborers in our country. An approach which is based primarily on *our own* perception of the needs and *our own* prescription for a solution, which does not pay close attention to what farm workers themselves are saying, is likely to be presumptive and patronizing.

(3) FARM WORKERS, LIKE OTHER WORKERS (INDEED, LIKE THEIR EMPLOYERS AND ALL THE REST OF US), WANT TO HAVE THE FREEDOM TO JOIN TOGETHER IN A MUTUALLY BENEFICIAL ASSOCIATION.

In unity there is strength. In California there have been state-supervised secret ballot union representation elections since 1975. In those elections farm workers have voted overwhelmingly for union representation. Any grower who doubts this ought to be willing to accept collective bargaining preceded by a supervised, secret ballot representation election.

(4) SOME PART OF THE CHURCH NEEDS TO BE PRESENT WITH FARM WORKERS AS THEY GO ABOUT THE DIFFICULT WORK OF ORGANIZING.

It is part of the mission of the church to be present with those who are the poorest workers in our society. The church seeks to affirm such a *ministry of presence and of servanthood,* be open to such a ministry, and give it support. This is not the work of the whole church, which is concerned about the liberation of every person. But some (small?) part of the church needs to be focused on the needs of farm workers. Why? Because farm workers are asking for such a ministry; and because the church needs it for its own sake, to fulfill the Gospel mandate to be present with and be in the service of the poor (Matthew 25).

(5) IN OUR WORLD, AN ETHIC OF LOVE DOES NOT CONFLICT WITH THE ACQUISITION OF POWER.

God in the metaphor of Scripture, is our Father and has created all that is. God has given us authority to subdue the earth (Genesis 1:28). God has sent the Son to us "in power" (Romans 1:4). No one who clearly perceives that he or she is a child of God willingly accepts the domination of "the principalities and power, the world rulers of this present darkness" (Ephesians 6:12). In fact, those men and women of the farm workers' movement are about the business we all should be about: reclaiming a fallen, corrupted creation (Romans 8:21).

(6) THE ROLE OF MEDIATOR IS NOT A PROPER ROLE FOR THE WHOLE CHURCH IN THE FARM WORKERS' STRUGGLE FOR LIBERATION.

Mediation implies an equality of bargaining power on both sides. Such an equality does not exist in the present struggle between the tiny farm workers' union on one side and the tremendous power of the agribusiness industry on the other. It is likely that conflict is a result of an inequality of power rather than a balance of power. Therefore the church is serving the interests of peace and justice by seeking ways to correct the power imbalance, i.e., supporting farm worker organizing efforts.

(7) THE SPECIFIC DEEDS OF INDIVIDUAL CHRISTIANS ARE IMPORTANT.

Each one of us has a special bond, which joins us to the farm workers. We actually take into our bodies the products of their hands. And we can move from a posture of concern to one of effective action. You can, right where you are, become part of a national network of persons who *accept responsibility for* bringing a measure of justice into the lives of farm workers. You can become informed about the current issues in the struggle. Then, after becoming informed you can take action. You can help develop a strategy (and get helpful ideas from others) about how your own church might become more involved.

The crux of the issue comes down to economic power. The major tool of economic power for farm workers is the boycotting of the products of companies who fail to bargain in good faith.

Our deepest convictions about life require that we take up the cause of the men, women and children who harvest our food, and make their cause our own. This cause holds out the promise of a life of hope, of joy and of purposeful labor.

For more information:

National Farm Worker Ministry
438 N. Skinker
St. Louis, MO 63130

314 726 6470
www.nfwm.org

POETS TO COME

I myself but write one or two indicative words for the future,

I but advance a moment only to wheel and hurry back in darkness.

I am a man who, sauntering along without fully stopping, turns a casual look upon you and then averts his face,

Leaving it to you to prove and define it,

Expecting the main things from you.

Walt Whitman

Inscriptions
Leaves of Grass

FARM WORKERS: FROM THE SHADOWS INTO THE LIGHT

"Those who labor in the earth are the chosen people of God, if ever He had a chosen people . . ." (Thomas Jefferson, Notes on Virginia) [1]

"There are times, you know, when I ask myself what I ever did to deserve a deal like this. You know what I mean? I mean I feel there must be someone who's decided you should live like this for something wrong that's been done." A farm worker on the East Coast Migrant Stream, father of six [2]

The ideology of racial supremacy has cast a long shadow far ahead of itself, extending into our own time and doubtless far into the future. These notions of superiority become most potent in an environment of forgetfulness of history. When permitted to flourish unhindered and unchallenged, racism is insidious both for the destruction it brings down upon its victims and also because of the subtlety by which these ideas and theories insinuate themselves into the matrix of beliefs and customs of peoples the world over.

The situation of farm workers provides a contemporary example of the distressing and pervasive impact which racial exclusivism has within our culture. For Christians, who accept responsibility for the renewal of God's creation, the issue is a critical one. This is so because those who position themselves against excluded and deprived persons are so often part of the life of the local and the institutional church. The issue is sociological as well as theological because middle class Christians are frequently disengaged from the living problems of impoverished people.

The issue is also thoroughly political because the jurisdiction of government has been broadened to cover virtually every aspect of modern life. Unless the sociological and political aspects of our culture are addressed, theological commentary amounts to little more than bells and whistles; the management of the engine is in other hands.

Short and Long Memory

For generations the dreams and hopes of people who pick the crops in America have been cruelly refuted by experience. Temporary quarters in rural slums, domination by cruel and unscrupulous labor contractors, the daily fear of deportation by government agents, and exclusion of oneself and one's children from health care and educational opportunities are both terrible and commonplace concerns for farm workers.[3] Certainly the situation of farm workers must be addressed by society as a whole, for no matter how hard farm laborers work in the fields, these harsh conditions do not change - because the forces which gave rise to these conditions are found elsewhere than in the fields. If churches and their members were not so far removed from all of this, we might be justified in referring to these conditions as urgent pastoral problems.

Government policy and economic practice in this area have a long if not venerable history and are rooted in patterns, which extend back into the colonial period of the nation. This point should be kept clearly in view as the debate continues regarding the nation's immigration policies. The frontiers of the United States have never been closed to agricultural workers for the very practical reason that the workers are essential to the health of the agricultural industry as a whole. Today, however, the workers are brought, or come on their own, for a season at a time rather than for a lifetime. In fact, the current political and economic climate demands that they leave as soon as the harvest is done.[4]

Since the United States is the greatest commercial empire that the world has yet known, it should not surprise anyone that many thousands of individuals make their way into the country by whatever means possible, legal and otherwise. And since the executive branch of the government is bound to enforce the immigration laws, it is common for government agents to seek out and chase down suspected "illegals" and subject them to incarceration and summary deportation. The current government practice of hunting laborers down and shipping them out of the country should not be thought of as a new and unsavory aberration in our national life. These policies and procedures are not some wild variety of weed, which has grownup while we were not paying attention.

Residual Slavery . . .

From the beginning, American agriculture has imported its laborers, drawing on the poor of the world for the essential tasks of planting and harvesting. On America's commercial farms in particular, people of color have always picked the crops. For more than two hundred years the South relied upon indentured and slave labor. George Washington, the eighteenth century Virginia planter and Episcopal vestryman, who conducted our national war for independence, was not interested in an economic revolution. General Washington had his reasons, over two hundred of them, which was the number of chattel slaves, including children, who lived and labored at Mount Vernon. This number does not encompass the indentured servants that he "purchased" for shorter periods of time before and after he was president.[5] I draw attention to George Washington not so that we may point a self-justifying finger at the morals of an earlier day. President Washington wanted to free his slaves, but he knew he could not and also survive economically. The system was in place.

With the passage of the Homestead Act of 1862 and the formal termination of slavery, the promise of farm land was held out to black freemen and women. Harriet Tubman sang at that time,

*Come along! Come along! Don't be alarmed!
Uncle Sam is rich enough to give you all a farm!*[6]

But the hoped-for land never materialized. Lacking capital, equipment, tools, management skills, and any training except agricultural, most blacks remained in or near the place of their emancipation. They lived out their lives amid the lingering passions, personal tragedies, and economic ruin of the defeated southern states. From an economic point of view, freed slaves in the South were deprived of any assured livelihood and were set adrift in a chaos of hostility and devastation. From a political point of view, the southern black population was placed by Reconstruction in a dangerous and ultimately false position. As William Lloyd Garrison said in 1864,

"Chattels personal may be instantly translated from the auction block into freemen; but when were they ever taken at the same time to the ballot box and invested with all political rights and immunities? According to the laws of development and progress, it is not practicable."[7]

Garrison's opinion demonstrates the ambivalence, which prevailed among even the most fervent abolitionists. It is little wonder that formal liberation of the southern slaves did not bring with it all the rights of citizenship. The farm labor system of today still reflects this ambivalence, as different standards are applied to this work force, which, if applied to others, would immediately be seen as unjust.

Freed women and men were unable to establish themselves as farmers or even as rural wage earners after the Civil War. Southern planters had no capital to pay regular wages, so a system of credit was devised which permitted agricultural production to be carried on. Former slaves were allowed to remain in their cabins and work as before on land which was "let" or "rented" to them, in expectation of a share of the crops. Frequently, the "settling up" at the end of the season or the calendar year produced no cash. As likely as not, the share cropper family would find themselves in debt to the planter. In this way a permanent class of laborers was created. As southern agriculture expanded into various commercial crops, thousands of share croppers and their families went "on the stream" to supplement their wages and retain possession of the little plots which they worked. From the perspective of the people who worked the land, the postbellum South greatly resembled the antebellum South; rural slums replaced the slave quarters; the crew leader became a stand-in for the overseer.

. . . And the Hacienda System

Just as residual slavery accounts for much of the current situation of farm workers in the South, colonial California has provided the pattern for farm labor-management relations in the West and Southwest. It all began with the enormous haciendas, which had developed from the land grants made by Spain to favored, well connected individuals. After California was taken from Mexico in 1849, these huge tracts, each comprising hundreds of thousands of acres of the best agricultural land in the state, were frequently passed on intact to other favored individuals. In many instances, fraudulent deeds and "floating" grants enabled speculators to gain control of enormous areas. In 1871 in California, 500 men were the owners of 8,600,000 acres.[8] One enterprising speculator even claimed title to the city of San Francisco. While this claim was ultimately rejected, the courts upheld most of the rest. Additional thousands of acres were granted to the railroads as alternate rights-of-way tracts. "Our land system," said Governor Haight, "seems to be mainly framed to facilitate the acquisition of large blocks of land by capitalists or corporations either as donations or at nominal prices."9

With the completion of the transcontinental railroad and the development of refrigerated railroad cars in the 1870s, something more than wheat and cattle could be produced. There was an urgent need for hands to work labor intensive crops, which were shipped to population centers back East. Large scale, "Bonanza" farming had arrived. And with its arrival there had to be found or created a new class of people. Thomas Jefferson's idealistic picture of the noble freeholders - a portrait which continues to represent the American farmer in the popular mind - has nothing in common with the requirements of the enormous California ranches of the late nineteenth and twentieth centuries. In order to be economically sound, these operations have depended upon the services of thousands of workers, imported and exported with the change of the seasons.

Farm Labor: A Rainbow Coalition

From the point of view of the native population of California the tidal wave of Anglo immigration amounted to a genocidal occupation of the Indian world. By the 1860s the indigenous laborers, who had worked the non-commercial Spanish haciendas were no longer available. In the absence of Indian farm workers, Chinese laborers, who bad been imported to build the railroads, were brought into the fields. Even though tile Chinese demonstrated great skill in the physically demanding jobs in the fields, and even though there is some evidence that the Chinese workers actually taught the California rancher a great deal about the art of cultivation, this arrangement could not last.[10]

Jobs were scarce for the Anglo settlers who were drawn to California by gold fever and the various other fevers which caused hundreds of thousands of people to walk across a continent. Anti-Chinese proposals became more and more attractive to the politicians of the period. Ordinances were passed which attempted to regulate or exclude Chinese people. In 1882, Congress responded by passing the first immigration exclusion act.[11]

The Depression of 1893 drove thousands of previously employed Anglo workers to the point of destitution. In rural California, homeless "settlers" often found themselves competing for jobs in the fields with "coolies." By the end of 1893, racial hostility had reached a murderous pitch. Thousands of Chinese were forced off their jobs and out of rural California by rioters who raided the fields and set fire to labor camps. The riots, which were motivated by racial exclusivism and which occurred throughout the agricultural areas of the state, permanently eliminated Chinese workers from the farm labor picture.

The loss of these workers fueled a debate which was already underway in west coast agricultural circles before the turn of the century.[12] The debate centered upon the issue of recruitment for the enormous commercial enterprises which had replaced the wheat farms of the post-Civil War era. The rigid economies of agribusiness required only a small year-round work force, but approximately ten times that number for a few weeks every year. Among the employers were those who advocated a labor procurement program with a social purpose - an invocation of the Jeffersonian ideal of the sturdy and independent farmer. It was argued that the solution to the grower's labor problems was the large scale recruitment of "the farmer lads of the agricultural districts of the Eastern States," who would both work the land and also help to populate the sparse agricultural regions of the state.[13] An advocate of this kind of labor recruitment program argued that "an intelligent, thrifty, energetic, steady, young white man who was raised on a farm can do more work than any laborer a fruit-grower can secure."[14]

Meanwhile, the same dogma of racial supremacy had led agricultural employers in the South to the opposite conclusion. Not only were people of color desirable farm workers, they were peculiarly qualified for this kind of employment. John W. Dubose of Birmingham, Alabama invoked Biblical imagery, in 1886, when he spoke of the advantages of "a large body of strong, hearty, active, docile and easily contented Negro laborers, who conform to the apostolic maxim of being "contented with their wages" and [have] no disposition to strike."[15] Two years later an Alabama planter said, "White labor is totally unsuited to our methods, our manners, and our accommodations." Who, then, is available for field work? "No other laborer [than the Negro] of whom I have any knowledge, would be as cheerful, or as contented on four pounds of meat and a peck of meal a week, in a little log cabin 14 x 16 feet, with cracks in it large enough to afford passage to a large sized cat."[16] With even more candor, another planter stated, "Give me the nigger every time. The nigger will never strike as long as you give him plenty to eat and half clothe him; he will live on less and do more hard work, when properly managed, than any other class or race of people."[17]

Shortly after the turn of the century, west coast agricultural circles had ended their debates about labor procurement and abandoned any efforts to develop a socially viable labor policy. Some attempt had been made to secure Anglo workers, but these recruitment drives were half hearted at best, since they compromised a fundamental business principle, the maximization of profits. Accordingly, the industry pushed ahead in its efforts to recruit foreign labor.[18] This approach brought the West Coast into conformity with the agricultural employment patterns in the South and East and coincided with American expansion overseas, particularly in the Philippines and the Caribbean. President McKinley's attitude is typical of the racial-religious pretensions, which were fashionable in America at the turn of the century. When McKinley asked God for guidance about what to do with the Philippines, God reportedly told him, "Take them."[19]

Having decided to pursue a labor recruitment program, which offered the greatest promise of profitability, but which contradicted the ideals of a few years before, agribusiness in California needed to develop a justification for the socially dysfunctional labor relations system to which it had become committed. The explanation was found in the racial myths, which are so frequently drawn upon at times of social dislocation and dissonance. Where once it was said that the best worker was the energetic and steady white farmer from the East, now it was maintained that non-white laborers are more naturally suited to field work. This is due, it was argued to "their relatively small stature, ability to tolerate hot weather, native stoicism, and innate lack of ambition."[2c] In 1929, an observer noted, "stoop crops, that require much bending over, like picking strawberries or cutting asparagus, the white laborer finds particularly tiring and is unwilling to handle. Such crops naturally tend to fall to races like Orientals, accustomed to squat rather than sit."[21] For the past four generations, then, in the South as well as in California and the Southwest, harvesting requirements have depended upon the temporary presence of voiceless, excluded minorities, imported and then exported with the change of the seasons.

After the Chinese were excluded from the fields, Japanese, then Filipino and Mexican laborers were imported specifically for short term harvesting needs. Using their political influence and working through various associations set up for the purpose, employers saw to it that government- sponsored labor procurement programs, were set up.

The rationale which supported foreign recruitment programs tended to rule out even the possibility of hiring white workers for field work. But of course, there were significant numbers of these workers. Accordingly, an explanation for this contradiction was found in the theories of social Darwinism, which were current seventy-five years ago. It was stated that the presence of these workers in the fields was due to natural selection. These workers were too "shiftless and irresponsible;" their "collective depravity" made them unfit for white man's work.[22] The farm labor population in the United States thus reflected the colors of the rainbow; and like a proper rainbow, should contain every color - but white.

Such notions served both to explain the existence of the non-white farm worker caste and also to blunt any criticism aimed at reform. Things could never be different, it was argued, because of the "nature" of the workers. They were unfit for any other kind of life. It followed, then, that any agitation among the workers themselves must have some other cause than a legitimate protest over deplorable conditions.

The Cry for Justice in the Fields

But there were protests, which took various forms. One of the earliest recorded work stoppages occurred in Louisiana in 1880. From the American Cyclopedia of that year we read:

"This was not an uprising of blacks against white, but one of employees against employers, in the parishes of St. James, St. John the Baptist, and St. Charles. During the month of March, Negroes went from plantation to plantation, requiring others who had not joined their movement to desist from work and to even leave these parishes. They rode about in armed bands, broke into cabins and frightened the inmates, took quiet laborers from their work in the fields and whipped them. Louisiana's Governor Wiltz issued a proclamation, but it had no effect on the rioters, and the militia was called out and sent to two or three points of disturbance. The ringleaders were arrested without bloodshed or difficulty and were brought to New Orleans, tried and imprisoned."[23]

On the West Coast, each successive group of farm laborers from the Chinese workers in the 1880s onward had tried to organize and had conducted strikes. But the first farm labor organizing effort to gain national attention occurred in 1913-14.

1910-1914 were years of great prosperity for agricultural employers. These were the "parity years," that period when farmers were considered to have gotten their fair income. Today, if there is a shortage or a surplus in a particular commodity, the federal government may step in and buy up crops or pay growers to reduce acreage. The object is to keep farm income near parity, that is, as near as possible to the 1914 income levels.

But the prosperity of commercial agriculture was not shared by the workers. In 1913, W. B. Durst, a hop grower in Wheatland, California, had advertised picking jobs for 2,800 workers when only 1,500 were needed. People came to Wheatland from all over the West. On one crew of 235 men, 27 nationalities were represented. The 1,000 destitute surplus workers could not move on and conditions at the camp were intolerable.

> "Tents were rented from Durst at 75 cents a week; workers were forced to use his store as he forbade local grocers to make deliveries; there were 9 outdoor toilets for 2,800 people; drinking water was not allowed in the fields, since Durst's cousin had a lemonade concession there, at 5 cents a glass; a relative also owned the lunchtime 'stew wagon.'"[24]

At a mass meeting in the camp, complaints and protests were loud and a sick baby was held up before the crowd. Sheriff's deputies moved into the crowd, shots were fired and a riot ensued, during which a district attorney, deputy sheriff, and two workers were killed. The national guard was called out all over California. This protest as well as subsequent ones had been led by a labor organization known as the Industrial Workers of the World. When the

I.W.W. stated its opposition to the First World War, its leadership was prosecuted under various criminal syndicalism laws, and the organization, never very stable, collapsed.

Farm Workers Excluded from NLRA Protection

The depression years brought even more hardship to the landless, migratory work force. Distress in the cities created enough pressure to pass remedial legislation, but the New Deal, which helped urban workers and farmers, had no effect upon the condition of farm workers. In fact, the National Labor Relations Act, known as the Wagner Act, was passed only after Southern legislators had been assured that agricultural workers and domestic servants would not be covered.

In the summer of 1933, there was a huge cotton surplus. The Agricultural Adjustment Act was passed that year and required that surplus cotton be plowed under in order to create scarcity and hold up prices. This policy destroyed the meager livelihoods of the sharecroppers, who could only be paid by bringing in a crop.

Clay East, a tenant farmer and early leader of the Southern Tenant Farmers Union (STFU) told of his reaction to a government agent who asked him what he thought. "I really blew up . . . he was asking me if I approved of people in rags with no sheets in the house plowing under cotton."[25] When the mules avoided stepping on the cotton which they were made to plow up, the tenants said, "Mules have more sense than men."[26] The union attempted to protest the deliberate destruction of the cotton crop by organizing cotton pickers, black and white, but the STFU was defeated by the weight of hostile government and community reaction, augmented by vigilantes, who broke up meetings and harassed local leaders. The STFU never succeeded in signing any contracts in agriculture.

Without the protective umbrella which NLRA coverage would have provided, farm labor organizing efforts could not succeed. However, the effort was made, especially in California, to organize the Dust Bowl immigrants from the central plains. In 1933 major strikes occurred in the Imperial Valley, the Salinas Valley and the great central valley of the San Joaquin, under the direction of the Cannery and Agricultural Workers International Union. The goal of this activity was to drive up depression wages and secure contracts. However, the strike leaders were arrested and sent to prison for violations of the state criminal syndicalism law while paramilitary Committees of Vigilance, which had come into existence in California as early as the 1850s, used threats and outright terror against the workers. Most notable of these vigilantes were the Associated Farmers, who were brutally successful in their efforts to discourage farm workers from organizing a union.[27]

The Bracero Program (1942-1964)

The Second World War created jobs in west coast war production industries for many of the Anglo Dust Bowl immigrants. Their place was taken in the fields by "*braceros*," laborers imported from Mexico under government contract. The importation programs were continued on a "temporary" basis for twenty years after WWII, justified by assertions of agricultural employers and the certification of the Secretary of Labor that "domestic" workers were unavailable or unwilling to do the work.

Worker importation programs had a devastating effect upon both farm workers and small farmers. In the words of Linda Lewis Tooni,

"With this cheap labor supply, the huge corporate farms not only depressed conditions for domestic workers, but also undercut small farmers in the marketplace by producing crops requiring more intensive

labor more cheaply than they could. California's share of agricultural production rose at the expense of everyone except the corporate farmers. The evils that result when the power is all on one side in a labor situation are nowhere more clearly demonstrated than here, where growers were able to secure large-scale government assistance in obtaining cheap foreign labor, while domestic farm workers had no voice powerful enough to defend their right to their jobs and livelihood." 28

Wages in agriculture on the West Coast were frozen for years because of the presence of braceros, who could not negotiate effectively for increases. Braceros were frequently used as strikebreakers against domestic workers, who found it impossible to organize or negotiate with their employers when there existed such a convenient source of cheap, manageable labor. Much the same picture existed - and still exists - in Florida and along the East Coast, where workers are imported under government supervision from Jamaica and Puerto Rico. Finally, in 1964, after years of protest by the labor movement, community and church groups, the Bracero Program was ended on the West Coast, and the way was cleared for the most successful farm labor organizing effort in history, an effort which was encouraged and supported by church workers who were closest to the farm workers, the California Migrant Ministry.

Farm Workers and the Protestant Churches

By and large, the response to the situation of farm workers by caring people - who are not themselves farm workers - can be placed on a continuum. The response begins with (1) sympathetic concern, focused on direct services to individuals followed by (2) agitation for remedial legislation, which in turn has been followed by (3) formal support for collective bargaining within the agricultural industry. This pattern can be seen both in the careers of individuals as well as in the developing work of Protestant migrant ministry programs.

In the 1920s the plight of farm workers came to the attention of Protestant church people, who responded in a systematic way. Under the leadership of church women in New Jersey, child care centers were established in eight labor camps.[29] Soon the work had expanded to other eastern states. Migrant Ministries, both denominational and ecumenical, began to take shape. For the next thirty years the programs of the various Migrant Ministries were refined, focusing largely upon labor camp visitation programs, recreational activities for the children, Sunday School classes and worship services. By the 1940s, still under the leadership of church women, Migrant Ministry programs existed in twenty-five states. The nationwide effort to develop and sustain a formal church presence with farm workers was being coordinated by the National Migrant Committee of the Home Mission Council of North America. The Home Mission Council came under the sponsorship of the then-new Division of Home Missions of the National Council of Churches in 1950.

Denominational outreach to farm workers was similar to the ecumenical Migrant Ministries, with the emphasis upon labor camp visitation. Clothing and food were distributed, and, in those areas where the migrant workers "wintered," there were special Thanksgiving dinners and Christmas parties for the children. At least one Migrant Ministry in the '50s made an effort, pathetic though it was, not to humiliate the people; toys were given first to the parents, who could then pass them on to the children.

But very little changed for farm workers as a result of all of this activity. The caste of laborers, "marked by the color badge of servitude,"[30] remained in their poverty, powerlessness, and isolation. From the New Deal onward there had been a parade of federal and state commissions which studied the situation, suggested remedies (restrictions on child labor, regulation of labor contractors, licensing of labor camps, increases in agricultural wages, inclusion of farm workers under workers compensation, inspection of crew buses, etc.) and then were disbanded. The staff of the various Migrant Ministries, working harder by the 1950s on remedial legislation, began to express their own frustration at the failure of politicians to address the plight of these workers and their families.[31]

Of course the people of the Migrant Ministry could not be at every camp. At best, their accidental presence could offer hope of only a temporary redress or improvement. Even those activities which focus upon remedial legislation tend to hint at patronizing agenda-setting: middle class people attempting to determine and win support for legislation directly affecting not themselves, but a deprived economic class, which is too weak to advocate for its own interests.

The collective bargaining process offers an important advantage in this respect, which is that the farm workers themselves, together with their employers, may take primary responsibility for this process and also for addressing and correcting defective labor/management relations. However, support for collective bargaining for farm labor unfortunately carries a great burden. In most parts of the United States, farm workers are as voiceless on this topic as they are on any other. And the agricultural industry is bitterly resistant to collective bargaining for farm workers because collective bargaining is an approach, which lays the ax to the root of the agribusiness labor-procurement system. Hostility to collective bargaining for farm workers is the cornerstone of agribusiness political activity in California today. The industry is mobilizing itself to weaken both the language as well as the administration of the state's landmark Agricultural Labor Relations Act. The only law of its kind, the ALBA mandates secret ballot elections and good faith bargaining to settle labor-management disputes.

It is at the point of transition from direct service and/or remedial solutions to empowerment where the middle class Christian is confronted with an acute dilemma. Standing with farm workers very likely means standing against the most influential individuals within the local church. For this reason, many churches are willing to offer financial support for direct service programs for farm workers but will have nothing to do with any program which is focused upon the empowerment of farm workers themselves.

Such a dilemma says much about the setting in life of many Christian churches today, which exist far from the periphery of society where human needs are the greatest. Even those denominations whose history is one of official dissent and repression at the hands of governmental authority are today very secure as to their finances and their respectable standing in the community. In this setting, the subject of collective bargaining for farm labor is hot indeed.

Still, the people of the Migrant Ministry found themselves drawn along by their concern for the human beings who appeared seasonally on the edges of their communities, moving from one rural slum to another, carrying their children and all their possessions with them. In spite of the risks, the churchmen and churchwoman of the Migrant Ministries, who love and serve their religious institutions, were compelled to ask and then try to answer a still recurring question: what needs to be done to *change permanently* the situation of farm workers in America?

Early, groping attempts to suggest answers can be traced in the back issues of *Western Harvest* published by the Migrant Ministry in California.[32] In 1949, there was no mention at all of the widely publicized strike at the DiGeorgio Corporation in Arvin, California; but in a later issue a San Joaquin cotton strike was reported as a news item, with favorable mention made of the increase in wages which the strike had won. By the late 50's, the newsletter was running articles entitled "Getting At the Roots," and publishing pictures of farm workers, mostly of *men*. Since the emphasis was no longer exclusively upon charitable activities, there was no need to focus upon women and children - as though there were no men in the work force at all.

The staff of the Migrant Ministry began to seek exposure to farm labor groups. In the rural counties of California, Migrant Ministry staff, who had some training in community organizing, began to join with labor and community groups in lobbying for increased services for farm workers, instead of trying to provide assistance through church channels.33 In 1960, *Western Harvest* made mention of "collective bargaining legislation" for farm workers.

The stage was set for a new phase in the work of the Migrant Ministry: explicit, direct support for farm workers who were attempting to build their own union and take part in collective bargaining with their employers. With the end of the Bracero program in 1964, this union building effort could begin.

1965-1970 *Controversy and Recognition*

In the spring of 1965, Filipino grape picking crews successfully struck for higher wages in the Coachella Valley of southern California. As the harvesting season moved north, the strike moved with it. In Delano, located in the great central valley, the Filipino workers continued their strike, which would be broken if Mexican crews did not join them.34

After initial hesitation and considerable discussion about strategy and timing, the Mexican crews voted to join the Filipinos on the picket line. For the Migrant Ministry, these events marked a change, a transformation in the way denominations and churches would be related to farm labor. Throughout the strike, which lasted through that season and several subsequent harvests, the staff of the California Migrant Ministry traveled up and down the state seeking financial support for the strikers, explaining farm labor issues from the workers' perspective and arguing forcefully that at least some part of the church needs to he present with workers who are seeking redress and greater control over their own lives.

From the CMM newsletter, June, 1965:

"Verbal truth telling is inadequate. Our deeds already speak louder than our words. The oppressed people of our society (farm workers among them) are alienated from our message for they see the Church as part of an established order which has kept them weak and poor and promises to do the same to their children

Evangelism is tough business. It is not to be spoken of lightly. It requires faithful witness which must mean taking our suffering brother seriously - seriously enough to be there with him, listen to his pain, to share our pain with him, to serve justice even when it is costly. The task is enough to humble us, to unite us and keep us busy for the days to come." [35]

This stance shattered the largely rural church constituency, which had supported the Migrant Ministry in its charitable activities. But through much hard work and many hours of meetings and talking with church people across the state of California, a new constituency was found in the urban areas. The California Migrant Ministry was able to sustain its funding, enlarge its staff, and, in 1971, transform itself into the National Farm Worker Ministry. Since then, the NFWM has stood with farm workers across the country, who are organizing their own union and seeking negotiations and contracts with agricultural employers. Throughout the 70s and 80s the NFWM has encouraged support for consumer boycott efforts, which farm workers have mounted against the products of companies who have been resistant to collective bargaining. Through effective, selfless organizing efforts, the United Farm Workers Union (UFW) has negotiated dozens of contracts which have increased wages and provided for health care and job security for thousands of farm workers in California. The Union also has a contract covering the citrus workers of Coca Cola in Florida.

At last, after many generations, the pattern of abuse and exclusion has begun to change for farm workers in America. And one small part of the church, at least, has been there with them and will continue to be there in the years ahead.

Racial Exclusvism and the Christian Faith

The situation of farm workers in America is symptomatic of the distressing and pervasive impact of racial exclusivism within our culture. I have attempted to show how this ideology has played a role in farm labor relations - both as a response to and as an argument against justice for farm workers.

However, against the ideology and the practice of racial exclusivism, the Christian faith offers a decisive rebuttal. Simply stated, racism in any form is not compatible with the faith that we profess. For this reason, the continuing distress of farm workers in the South and West is both a human condition of suffering which demands redress and also a moral dilemma confronting the churches of the nation. An argument can be made that the Christians of the South face a particularly compelling challenge in this respect.

On the whole, church organizations have not adequately addressed the economic motives or the racial justifications, which have determined the shape of labor-management relations in commercial agriculture. All too often, appeals from farm workers or from the people of the Migrant Ministry are met by indifference or even hostility by many within the churches who indicate that "the church" should be "neutral" in labor-management disputes. A posture of non-involvement is too easily given a borrowed dignity with the Pauline theme of reconciliation. Silent acquiescence to economic power does no credit to the liberating Gospel of Christ.

Time and again, Paul the Apostle to the "*ethne*" (*the peoples* or *the nations*; or better, anybody and everybody) insisted that neither racial nor ethnic differences nor divergent religious or cultural practice should become a condition for entrance into the house-churches he established.³⁶ Repeatedly he urged his converts not to permit racial exclusivism to determine their relations with one another; the God Paul serves is the Creator of all there is. "Having begun with the Spirit, are you now ending with the flesh?" (Gal. 3:3). "There is neither Jew nor Greek, there is neither slave nor free, there is neither male nor female; for you all are one in Christ Jesus" (Gal. 3:28). "For in Christ Jesus, neither circumcision nor un-circumcision is of any avail - but faith working through love" (Gal. 5:6).

We do well to keep in view the cosmic horizons of our faith, which Paul stresses with great force, especially in Romans.³⁷ Indeed, we do possess a socio-political mandate to renew and transform God's world ". . . *for the creation itself will be set free from its bondage to corruption and receive the splendid liberation of the children of God.*" (Rom. 8:21)

NOTES

1. Cletus E. Daniel, *Bitter Harvest, A History of California Farm Workers, 1870-1941*, (Ithaca: Cornell University Press, 1981), p. 15.
2. Quoted in Robert Coles, *Uprooted Children,* (New York: Harper and Row, 1970), p. 65.
3. Current literature detailing farm labor conditions is extensive. See Ronald L. Goldfarb, A *Caste of Despair* (Ames: The Iowa State University Press, 1981); Statements by Jerome Cohen, et al., *Farm Worker Collective Bargaining,* U.S. Government Printing Office, 1979, pp. 142-143; Ronald B. Taylor, *Sweatshops in the* Sun (Boston: Beacon Press, 1973); "Promises to Keep: The Continuing Crisis in the Education of Migrant Children," National Child Labor Committee, 1972; Senate Committee on Labor and Public Welfare, Subcommittee on Health and Subcommittee on Migratory Labor, *Joint Hearings,* 1972; "Migrant Farm Workers in North Carolina," Report by the Migrant Ministry Committee, North Carolina Council of Churches (Raleigh, 1982); Jacques Levy, *Cesar Chavez, Autobiography of La Causa* (New York: W. W. Norton, 1975). For an excellent bibliography of materials published before 1974, see Beverly Fodell, *Cesar Chavez and the United Farm Workers, A Selective Bibliography* (Detroit: Wayne State University Press, 1974), 104 pages.
4. [Note written in 1984] Congress is presently working on a major immigration bill. Known as the Simpson-Mazzoli Bill, the measure is a mixed bag of provisions, which indicates the uncertainty with which our immigrant nation addresses this issue. Passed by the House and the Senate in two different forms, the measure was opposed in this election year by both presidential candidates. Its chief sponsors do not represent areas greatly impacted by immigrants but suggest the bill will help mainly Hispanic immigrants. However, Simpson-Mazzoli is opposed by most Hispanic organizations. The bill contains complicated

documentation procedures for unregistered aliens as well as a provision reinstating a farm worker importation program, which was terminated and discredited twenty years ago. Touted as an attempt to "regain control" of the nation's southern border, the bill mandates no additional funds to accomplish this and appears to be little more than an effort to restore greater control to employers over agricultural workers.

5. Marcus Cunliffe, *George Washington, Man and Monument* (New York: New American Library, 1982), p. 104.
6. *With These Hands, Women Working on the Land,* edited by Joan M. Jensen (New York: The Feminist Press, McGraw Hill, 1981), p. 96.
7. Quoted in C. Vann Woodward, *The Burden of Southern History* (New York: Random House, 1960), pp. 89-90.
8. Carey McWilliams, *Factories in the Field* (Santa Barbara: Peregrine Smith, 1971), p. 20.
9. Ibid. p. 21.
10. Ibid. p. 71.
11. See McWilliams, ibid. pp. 66-80 and also *California, The Great Exception* (New York: A. A. Wyn, 1949), pp. 127-170.
12. Daniel, *op. cit.,* pp. 40-70.
13. Ibid., P. 51.
14. Ibid., P. 52.
15. Quoted in C. Vann Woodward, *Origins of the New South, 1877-1913* (Baton Rouge: Louisiana State University Press, 1967), p. 221.
16. A. W. S. Daniel, quoted in Woodward, ibid., p. 208.
17. Ibid., p. 208. The speaker is not identified.
18. Daniel, *op. cit.,* pp. 60-70.
19. President McKinley in an 1898 address to ministers at the White House: "I went down on my knees and thanked to God Almighty for light and guidance. And late one night it came to me this way. I don't know how it was but it came . . . . . There was nothing left to do but take them all and to educate the Filipinos and civilize and Christianize them . . .

." Quoted in Howard Zinn, A *People's History of the United States* (New York, Harper and Row, 1980), pp. 305-306.
20. Daniels, *op. cit.,* p. 73.
21. Edward L Munson, "Solving the Farm Labor Problem in California," *Overland Monthly,* May, 1929, P. 37.
22. Daniel, *op. cit.,* p. 73.
23. Quoted in H. L. Mitchell, *Mean Things Happening in This Land* (Montclair: Allanheld Osmun, 1979), pp. 284-285.
24. Linda Lewis Tooni, *Farm Labor Organizing, 1905-1967* (New York: National Advisory Committee on Farm Labor, 1967), p. 13.
25. Ibid., pp. 19-20.
26. Ibid., p. 20.
27. Daniel, *op. cit.,* p. 141; also McWilliams, *Factories,* ibid., pp. 211-229.
28. Tooni, *op. cit.,* p., 35.
29. For the outline of church work with farm workers, 1920 to the 1980s, I have drawn upon the files of the National Farm Worker Ministry. II I-A Fairmont Avenue, Oakland, CA 94611.
30. Beard, Charles A. and Mary B. Beard, *Basic History of the United States* (New York: Doubleday, 1944), p. 288.
31. After working behind the scenes with Congressmen Richard Nixon, Thomas Werdel, and Thruston Morton to discredit a fledgling farm labor organizing effort in 1950, Congressman Tom Steed was unusually candid. Sympathy for farm workers, he said, "was just the wrong view for me, and certainly wasn't the sort of thing I could go along with and still expect to survive politically in my district." Quoted in Ernesto Galarza, *Spiders in the House and Workers in the Field* (Notre Dame: University of Notre Dame Press, 1970), p. 160.
32. See note 29.
33. Carl Tjerandsen, *Education for Citizenship, A Foundation's Experience* (1980: Emil Schwarzhaupt Foundation, 425 Miramar Drive, Santa Cruz, CA 95060), pp. 439-447. This book is a report from the Foundation "on

what it did with the funds at its disposal and on what results were observed." The book belongs in every seminary and university library and is available *free of charge.*
34. For the history of the Delano strike, see John Gregory Dunne, *Delano, The Story of the California Grape Strike* (New York: Farrar, Straus, and Giroux, 1967).
35. The *California Migrant Ministry Newsletter* was the successor to *Western Harvest.*
36. Rom. 14; I Cor. 7:17-20; I Cor. 8; I Cor. 9:19-23; 2 Coy. 3:17; Cal. 5:1, 6, 13-15.
37. Especially but not exclusively Rom. 1.14-2:11, 5:1-6; 8:18-39.

91, IN HOSPICE

Awake, she ate with unexpected haste

Hands flying over the tray spilling nothing

Coffee is stone cold, she said to the room

Ignoring the gloved hand caressing her hair

RBC

THE FIRST AMENDMENT AND RELIGION

"Congress Shall Make No Law Respecting An Establishment of Religion, or Prohibiting the Free Exercise Thereof"

Responding to military successes after his armies painted Christian symbols upon their shields, the Roman emperor Constantine in the fourth century A.D. ordered that citizenship and church membership were to be coextensive. This church-state tie was severed in 1791 with the passage of the remarkable First Amendment to the United States Constitution. In the words of the historian Philip Schaff, a civil government, for the first time in history, deprived itself "of all legislative control over religion." What factors brought about this reversal in America of fourteen hundred years of church-state relations? What importance does the First Amendment have today?

THE RATIONALIST STANCE OF THE FRAMERS: FREEDOM OF THOUGHT IN MATTERS OF RELIGION

Many devout Americans such as John Jay and Luther Martin played important roles in the adoption of the Constitution and the first ten amendments. However, many of the most influential and politically active colonial leaders in the 1780s thought of themselves as religious dissenters or rationalists. Such American statesmen as Franklin, Jefferson, and Madison responded intellectually to religious questions by formulating a set of principles whereby the existence of God could be demonstrated or logically debated. These American rationalists wished to draw on religious impulses for their social benefits - not because religion is ultimately true or important but because it is useful in maintaining public order. They were willing to promote religion not for any intrinsic value it may have but in the interest of cohesion in public and social life.

However, these articulate and vastly influential intellectuals were critical of any and all churches sanctioned by the state - both the Congregational establishment in New England and the established Anglican church in Virginia. Insisting on the sanctity of the intellect, they were hostile to what they considered the coercive practices of all official "established" churches. Rationalist dissenters considered the right to private judgments concerning religious truth an "inalienable" right; that is, a right of the individual that can neither be taken away nor given up. Arguing that religious conviction is subject only to the private judgment of each person, these rationalists meant to ensure that the new American government, unlike virtually every European state, would be constitutionally forbidden from imposing religious practices upon any citizen.

AMERICAN RELIGIOUS PRACTICE IN THE 1780s: FROM ESTABLISHMENT TO TOLERATION

Apart from the already mentioned established churches there existed a number of churches that were not sponsored by any colonial government. Rooted in European traditions, these churches endorsed the civil enforcement of religious practices. Among these, the Presbyterian and Lutheran bodies joined with the established churches in advocating uniformity of religious practice as a matter of principle. However, many conformist ministers recognized the pluralistic nature of the American church scene and became advocates of toleration. Other religious groups, including Baptists and Quakers, rejected conformity in matters of religion and insisted that government must not favor one religious "establishment" and hinder others. These sects, which were active on the American frontier and growing rapidly because of revivalist movements, were weakening both established and conformist churches.

For practical reasons, frontier sects made common cause with the rationalist political leadership of the young nation. Working in concert to mobilize public opinion, their goal was to legalize religious freedom as the best means to protect it for all. In summary, the successful push for religious freedom in the constitutive legal document of the new nation was a positive rationalist and sectarian thrust. This achievement was based on practical self-interest and appealed above all to the principle of voluntarism in matters of religious practice.

THE AFTERMATH: A BREACH CAUSED BY REVEALED TRUTH AND ROBESPIERRE

The sectarian and rationalist alliance crumbled within a generation of the adoption of the First Amendment. The reason for the rupture was a serious disagreement about the source of truth. Eighteenth-century rationalists held then and humanists would maintain today that the mind is sufficient to discover truth. Devout Americans, whether conformists or sectarians, held that revelation is essential to knowledge of the truth of faith and were suspicious of any view which declined to acknowledge a decisive role played by God as Source of ultimate truth. Devout citizens today, whether liberal or fundamentalist, likely would agree with one another and with their eighteenth-century counterparts on this point.

The first great breach between rationalist politicians and their religious allies was caused by the French Revolution. In the view of many American religious leaders of various traditions, the disaster that overwhelmed France at the close of the eighteenth century was the direct result of rationalist and romantic notions about the self-sufficient perfectibility of humankind. To many devout Americans, it was clear that such convictions lead naturally to murderous excess. From countless

American pulpits, the argument was made that rationalism tends toward personal immorality and social chaos. Thomas Jefferson, attacked as an "infidel," countered by urging that the states follow the federal Constitution and disestablish all religious organizations.

After their brief political alliance with rationalist dissenters in the 1780s Baptists, Methodists, and other sectarians - together with the old establishment and conformist churches - built themselves in the nineteenth century into the uniquely American church organization: the denomination. There can be little doubt that the remarkable growth of American denominations would not have occurred in the nineteenth century but for the antiestablishment impulses of the First Amendment framers, which gave the various sects room to grow. The development of denominations has meant that by the mid-twentieth century the role of the devout citizen has changed. No longer a sectarian but a member of an influential denomination, the Baptist, Methodist, Reformed, Disciple might join with the heirs of majoritarian conformism (Presbyterians, Lutherans) and the heirs of the established churches (Episcopalian, Congregational, Roman Catholic) and reconsider American church history with a greater appreciation for the value to each of the disestablishment clause of the First Amendment.

With acknowledgment to the historian Sidney Mead,[1] one might summarize these events as a parable. A rationalist and sectarian marriage built the First Amendment in 1791 as a house for all Americans. The sectarian shortly obtained a divorce and quickly remarried Protestant orthodoxy. The new couple produced many denominations. The offspring of the second couple continue to live in the house built during the first marriage. However, some of the children occasionally declare their unwillingness to maintain the house or announce their desire to remodel it.

CONTINUING RELIGIOUS ISSUES

It may be instructive to look at contemporary church-state issues in light of the religious establishment struggle of the 1780s and the subsequent fragmentation of the rationalist/sectarian alliance.

*Non-establishment – **Not** Separation of Church and State*

First of all, "non-establishment" is a better formula than "separation of church and state" for understanding and describing the aims and achievements of the First Amendment framers. Drafted by a committee of the first Congress, then passed by Congress and ratified by the states in 1791, the First Amendment *specifically addresses the non-establishment of religious bodies - not the separation of church and state.* There is in fact no separation of church and state in any practical sense in America. Unlike church members in many other nations, in the United States church members and even church officials may vote and hold elective office and exercise all the rights and responsibilities of citizenship. Church bodies may seek to influence government in various ways, operate a variety of institutions, incorporate, own property and even enjoy tax exemptions extended to them by government. *The essence of the First Amendment revolution is not church-state separation but the rejection of coercion in favor of persuasion in matters of religion.*

Neo-conformism and the First Amendment

Finally, there are aspects of the current church-state debate that look familiar in light of the rationalist / sectarian alliance and the subsequent realignment of sectarianism with the old established churches. In other words, during the constitution writing and ratification period, Baptists and other separatists joined with Thomas Jefferson to disestablish the government sponsored churches of the colonial period. Then, seeking to impose a generalized Christian conformity upon civil society, these separatists allied with the now disestablished churches to attack federal authority and Jefferson in particular as an infidel for failing to give official preference to Christian practice. The ongoing debates about whether and to what extent government ought to defer to one or another church-endorsed policy (such as proscribed school prayer, the criminalization of abortion, genetic research) are extensions of the eighteenth-century issue of government preference for a particular religious establishment. Aren't these arguments a replay of the 1790's attempt by devout Americans first to refute the rationalists about the locus of truth and then equate rationalism with depravity?

Today's advocates of governments-enforced conformity disregard the essence of what the framers, in a majority, agreed upon: religious pluralism is an integral feature of the American scene. It should never be forgotten that not only sectarians but also church leaders from every tradition worked for passage of the First Amendment as a protection of the religious freedoms of all.

Every effort to use civil and especially prosecutorial government power to enforce uniformity of religious practice must be measured against the fact that a religious consensus does not and cannot exist in America. Civil government today cannot mandate or even advocate religious observances or policies on religious grounds, without coercing some minority perspective. All who wish to invoke civil power in the interest of religious truth, who wish others to become neo-conformists or who wish to create a neo-establishment of their own design should be reminded that the Constitution and our subsequent history have closed the door on religious conformity in the United States.

1. Sidney E Mead, **THE LIVELY EXPERIMENT** (New York: Harper & Row (1963) p. 38.

MAL CAMINO MAL DESTINO

No longer permitted to practice law, I wait to one side. My crimes: demands to a miscreant judge to step aside; confidential complaints to supervising judges; an aborted inquiry into the miscreant's ties to lawyers with court business - blocked by the miscreant. My many convictions: interference with the administration of "justice" by the miscreant; burdening lawyer-witnesses, whom guardians of judicial privilege decline to examine.

Questions which stop the ears of the guardians: How many judges receive money gifts from parties with court business? How many do favors in return? How many such judges are too many? One hundred? Ten? One? Not so few as one. Better to blacken the reputation of an officer of the court than to admit to one.

An information asymmetry: the robed miscreant accepts the gift(s) and does the judicial favor(s). The imprudent court officer denounces the miscreant. One is *distinguished*; one is tossed out of the miscreant *profession*. What is professed, thereby?

When the conduct of a robed miscreant is placed in issue, plenary investigative tools (under the control of judges) become as flaccid and useless as a third nipple. You states, whose judges punish lawyers for not gifting them. Your Counsels of Discipline blend the power of lions with the prestige of dung beetles. What are they afraid of? Judicial spite? What do they know that we cannot know? That gifts and favors to/from a robed miscreant are routine?

No Gifts Accepted - All Gifts Returned. This was the Cardozo Rule. The road from Benjamin Cardozo to this moment has been a long, downward strut and shuffle.

I have nothing but respect for the judges. Nothing. That's the problem.

RBC

OVER THE CARNAGE ROSE A PROPHETIC VOICE

. . .

(Were you looking to be held together by lawyers?
Or by an agreement on a paper?
Or by arms?
Nay, nor the world, nor any living thing will so cohere.)

Walt Whitman

Drum-Taps
Leaves of Grass

PAUL AND THE VICTIMS OF HIS PERSECUTION: THE OPPONENTS IN GALATIA

The Apostle Paul was known as a persecutor of Christians before his conversion to the very faith he attempted to suppress. (Gal 1:13; I Cor. 15:9; Phil. 3:6) What happened to Paul's victims? For two millennia, (A) the existence of Paul's victims and (B) their likely denunciation of him have escaped inquiry by the commentators and scholars, who have examined his letters.

The suggestions which follow are focused on what can be learned and inferred about the victims from Paul's own comments in the document he dictated (Gal 6:11) and which he directed "to the churches [assemblies/gatherings, *ekklesiai*] in Galatia" (Gal 1:1). This proposal does not require a conclusion (impossible to reach) as to whether the letter was ever received and read by its intended recipients.

Galatia is understood by this writer to refer to Anatolian Celtica, that is, the Celtic-populated region of Turkey, whose center is present day Ankara. Lightfoot[1], quoting Jerome, points out that this region was known earlier as "Gallo Grecia," reflecting the Celtic settlements in Asia minor in the third century BCE. A decision for the tribal locale excludes the possibility that Paul was referring to the later-named Roman province of "Galatia," which encompasses a larger area, taking in both the Celtic population as well as other tribal groupings to the Anatolian south, all the way to the Mediterranean Sea. It is unlikely, following Martyn, *contra* Dunn[2], Paul could have referred (Gal 3:1) disparagingly to various tribes in the Roman province as (my translation): "You stupid Celts!" Both Calvin and Luther were more attentive to the findings of ancient historians; Luther concluded,[3] Paul "calls them by the name that was proper to their country."

Modern uncertainty about the location of "the churches in Galatia" (Gal 1:1) has resulted from attempts to create a chronology of Paul's activities too greatly influenced by Acts (Meeks).[4] In addition to confirming the presence of Celtic tribes in Asia Minor (see comments, *supra*) Jerome, writing in the Fourth Century of the Common Era, stated that the Celts (Galatians) spoke both Greek and a language akin to that of a Celtic clan (the Treveri), who had settled centuries earlier in Roman Gaul (cited by Lightfoot).[5] Maintaining their identity long after Paul, the Celts of Anatolia were the addressees of his letter.

The thesis here proposed is that Paul was confronted in Galatia by accusations brought against him by some of his own victims; they may or may not have remained adherents of Messiah Jesus after suffering persecution at Paul's hands. Contrary suggestions through the centuries as to the identities of Paul's opponents in Galatia have been many and varied. The following antagonists have been proposed and maligned to one degree or another: competing missionaries affiliated with respected Judean believers (Dunn)[6], competing "teachers" (Martyn[7] following Aquinas[8] ["false teachers"]), Luther[9] ["teacher of works"], and Burton[10] ["teachers"]) (who also, with R. Bultmann, identified Paul's antagonists as "Judaisers"), "innovators" (Lightfoot)[11], "false apostles" (Luther)[12], some of Paul's own Celtic converts, who veered into "heresy" (Munck)[13]. In recent years, speculations about the identities of Paul's antagonists in Galatia have become increasingly nuanced and complex, carrying Paul and his Celtic converts far into the hermeneutical deep. Räisänen[14] posits belated "restorers" of Christian "orthodoxy." Or perhaps the difficulties may be traced to figures in local synagogues who wished either to "influence" (Nanos)[15] or "pressure" (Esler)[16] Paul's recent recruits into getting themselves circumcised.

All of the suggestions presuppose theologically sophisticated competitors to Paul, that is, Torah-oriented zealots who, for reasons of their own, wished to thwart Paul or undermine the thrust of his missionary work. The scholars appear to be holding a mirror to the text. Just as misleading as the assumption of theological sophistication on the part of Paul's critics, the commentaries posit an aggressive, law observant initiative directed to Gentiles by Jewish adherents of Messiah Jesus.

Such conjectures do not seem to represent a great advance in understanding Galatians. It is no longer possible to impute a program of proselytism to Diaspora Judaism. If Diaspora Judaism of this period was not a religion of colporteurs, why would a Messianic sect have been any different? There were proselytes to be sure, but there is scant evidence that Diaspora Judaism operated in any sense as a missionary religion. There did exist a so-called *Gentile mission* in the Diaspora undertaken by messianists who proclaimed Jesus as Messiah, a movement to which Paul became attached. This mission was aggressive but was not inclined to impose Torah observance upon Gentile adherents.

Gruen has recently summarized the present state of our knowledge about Jewish attitudes towards Gentiles. Evaluating the statements of Tacitus and Juvenal, Gruen suggests that Jews were notable for "keeping themselves entirely separate from other peoples and even shunning their company. It would not be easy to proselytize among the Gentiles if one were shunning their company!"[17] "In sum," he concludes, "conversion, missionary activity or proselytizing of any kind, do not appear as a source of concern."[18]

Similar findings were reached a decade earlier by McKnight, who considered evidence relevant both to the Diaspora and to Palestine: "Judaism never developed a clear mission to the Gentiles that had as its goal, the conversion of the world. Further, although there may have been a few 'evangelists' scattered throughout Jewish history, and although Jewish missionary activity may have existed at times in Rome, there is no evidence that could lead to the conclusion that Judaism was a 'missionary religion' in the sense of aggressive attempts to convert Gentiles or in the sense of self-identity."[19] There having been no first century Jewish missionary activity of any significance, and therefore, no circumcising mission, no basis exists for the additional imputation of a law-observant requirement of Gentiles, who are the targets of Diaspora Jews for belief in Messiah Jesus[20]

In addition to the isolated case of the proselyte, there were efforts within Judaism to establish ground rules for dealing with pious individuals, who wanted to associate themselves with Judaism in some manner. These individuals, possibly referred to as "God-fearers," were admiring of Judaism but not proselytes.[21] No doubt, Jews wished for good relations with such persons but there existed no Jewish campaign to reach out to Gentiles and bring them into Judaism. Simply put: Judaism did not recruit Gentiles. A reassessment of Paul's response to his antagonists in Anatolian Celtica is in order.

In the letter to the Galatians, Paul is responding to personal attacks made against him. So Lightfoot concluded (1865).[22] This insight is sound and should inspire caution in any who want to find a "center" or a "system" in Paul's letters. A century ago Wrede[23] (cited with approval by Esler)[24] correctly observed that Paul's "doctrine of justification by faith" is a "polemical doctrine" which is "made intelligible" only "by the struggle of his life." Burton[25], writing not long after Wrede, detected a "personal element" which was more likely than any doctrinal controversy to "cause embitterment" in Paul. The clearly "personal element" in the letter has been questioned recently by Nanos[26] but this interpretation of the letter is dependent upon a reading of Gal 1:1 as "vague."[27] Paul's white hot rage is anything but vague.

The attempts to find a system in Paul have been impressive. Käsemann,[28] notably followed by Martyn[29] who dedicated his commentary to Käsemann, sees "justification" ("rectification" in Martyn) as more central to Paul's thought than do Wrede and Schweitzer. Both Käsemann and Martyn appear to follow Bultmann's lead in their attempts to discern coherence in Paul. It is telling that Bultmann had difficulty fitting Galatians into his system. Bultmann concluded[30] Gal. 1:7 and 4:21 are exceptions to the anthropological categories he detected in

Paul. These texts, Bultmann asserts point to "the failure" of Paul's addressees "to perceive an exclusive antinomy" between law and grace. This "antinomy," according to Bultmann, required for Paul the rejection of "law" as no longer available to regulate the activities of human beings. Bultmann is discussing Galatians but seems to have Romans in mind, for Paul in Galatians expressed (Gal 2:21b; 3:19-26) a far more sweeping critique of the law. Paul took a more moderate view in his letter to the believers in Rome. (See Ro 5:20, 7:7-12). According to our thesis, Paul's conclusion in Galatians that Torah observance is inherently noxious was stated in defensive reaction to the denunciations of Paul by some of his victims. This circumstance did not recur when he wrote to the church in Rome.

The fact is, none of the scholars, whether they organize Paul's letter thematically or take a contextual approach, seem to have examined Paul's apologetic comments with his victims in mind. Nor have they considered the possibility that it was the victims who caused difficulties for Paul in the churches. To put the present proposal clear: Paul was confronted in the assemblies in Galatia by the credible accusations of victims of his earlier persecution of Christian Jews. This explains why some of Paul's comments are contradictory, as Paul piled arguments one upon the other to deflect their denunciations.

In his letter, Paul responded to accusations by a brief admission (Gal 1:13) which had been both preceded and followed by a defense (the balance of the letter) against charges made. By virtue of his professed allegiance to the executed Messiah, Paul argues that he now partakes of an apocalyptic victory. The indices of this victory include the reception into the heart of the Spirit of the Son (Gal 3:2-5; 4:6) and the abrogation of the dictates of Torah (Gal 2:16; 3:16; 5:11) and of all other legal strictures (Gal 3:23-25; 4:8-9; 5:1).

Note that for Paul, the Messiah was *lawfully* put to death, that is executed, with crucifixion the method (Gal

3:1; 4:4). This perspective enables Paul to condemn the law. His argument is, in effect, an argument for impunity from censure of any kind (Gal 2:21). Paul asserts that he will not permit himself to be subjected to judgment for his past misconduct (Gal 2:18) under a legal system which had played a limited (Gal 3:19) but crucial (Gal 3:23-26) role in the condemnation and execution of the Messiah. In this way, Paul argues that he cannot be judged by standards, which give standing to persecution victims (Gal 4:29-30). As discussed, *infra*, Paul's arguments, whether taken as a denigration of Torah or "the law" as applied to Gentiles, are idiosyncratic, going far beyond what we know of opinions clearly within Judaism or within the so called "Gentile Mission" which predated Paul.

Paul's generalized derogation of "law" suggests that his victims may not have charged him with any specific violation(s) of Torah. Instead, Paul may have been accused of failing to live up to the high moral standards and an attendant humane code of conduct which Judaism of this period was thought, in much of the Gentile world, to uphold. The suffering of victims, the reaction of their persecutors and the empathy which victims can elicit, cannot be seen from only one angle. Paul's response was to focus his defense on "the law" which, he insisted, can no longer be applied to his conduct.

But what about Gal 1:22-24? Paul states explicitly that the Judean churches "in Christ" who had been subjected to persecution, did not know Paul personally and thanked God for him, once he joined the ranks of the believers and began to proclaim the crucified Messiah. How can it be that such people subsequently denounced Paul? My answer is that the Judean believers were not the persecution victims who denounced Paul in Anatolian Celtica. These Judeans, combining Torah observance with belief in a Messiah, probably were not subjected to persecution at all. If this was the case, Paul could have been an abuser of some (i.e., Diaspora Jews on pilgrimage to Jerusalem) while remaining unknown personally to others (i.e., resident Judeans). These Judean believers having escaped a direct encounter with Paul, indeed, not even having been targeted by Paul, could be characterized later as praising God for him.

The Surface Meaning of a Text - even Scripture - is Suspect

By tradition and then by formal designation, Paul's letter to the Galatian assemblies has been taken as Scripture. In this capacity, the document has achieved a pre-eminent authority, by which it has brought solace to uncounted generations of believers. But an essential task of the commentator, with pretensions to scientific analysis, is to achieve transparency of the pre-literary situation. This procedure must begin with a suspicion of statements, even those statements, taken as Scripture.

Suspicion of the text achieved status as an interpretative principal in the 20th century. This development came about primarily through the influence of Heidegger and those theologians (e.g. Bultmann) and philosophers (e.g. Gadamer) who followed his two-fold hermeneutic program of (1) eschewing deduction for description and (2) distinguishing between "objective" inquiries and insights obtained by emotional, i.e., existential, or participatory inquiries.[31] The activities of textual critics influenced by this approach have entailed a search for a method of identifying the form of the text and clarifying its inner meaning, as opposed to its explicit meaning.[32] With this background, literary criticism, including an explication of the forms of ancient rhetoric, has become increasingly important as modes of evaluating texts deemed to be Scripture.

A question currently debated among today's scholars is: do the rhetorical techniques employed by Paul shed light on the meaning(s) to be found in the text of his letter? A valuable summary of the conclusions reached by applying rhetorical analysis to the letter to the Galatians has been made by Mack,[33] who identified a "pattern of rhetorical speech" therein. Betz[34] preceded Mack in arguing that Paul constructed his letter following rhetorical techniques. Betz has not been surpassed in the comprehensive treatment of the letter along the lines of rhetorical interpretation. However, an excessive emphasis upon rhetorical techniques as the key to the interpretation of Galatians can create problems of its own. Nanos for example wants to see[35] in Paul's rhetoric a single category, "irony." But Nanos' reduction loses traction because he does not come to terms with either Betz' or Mack's identification of a variety of rhetorical categories in the letter.

Efforts to classify the letter by resort to the categories of rhetoric known in the ancient world should proceed with considerable circumspection. It is not clear how these categories of oral communication precisely apply to the practice of letter-writing, as Esler[36] has shown. Kuula[37] also is cautious about centering the interpretation of Galatians around rhetorical categories, because "we are analyzing a letter which is read aloud by someone other than the writer." Mack concludes Galatians "unfolds, nonetheless, on the pattern of a rhetorical speech."[38] A rhetorical "pattern" may be there, but for our present purpose, it is enough simply to acknowledge that Paul was engaged in a responsive polemic (Gal 1:1; 1:20; 2:6, 6:17). As stated, the present proposal suggests this polemic was stimulated by denunciations made against Paul by former persecution victims.

The recognition of a polemic in the text triggers the search for the pre-literary context of the letter. If a pre-literary inquiry is not undertaken, commentary may assign a certain "meaning" to the text but at the risk of a premature contemporizing of the text and at the cost of becoming a hermeneutics of vindication. A vindicating embrace of the text is warranted by theological, devotional or ecclesiastic concerns, which arise subsequent to and outside of a text, held to be Scripture. But an uncritical approach to a text is not warranted by historical concerns, in so far as this embrace contributes to a loss of awareness of important aspects of the situation, which gave rise to the text.

The failure to consider and possibly even to hear the voices of Paul's victims has permitted Paul's defensive, idiosyncratic and anti-nomian polemic[39] to be seen not so much as an aspect of his argument but as the lynch pin of a theology, which stresses "faith" *against* "works." The contra-positioning of faith vs. works has been taken, improperly, as grounds for the denigration of Judaism as a superficial, legalistic system. The Reformation juxtaposition of faith and works has been undermined, as we have seen, by commentators of a hundred years ago (Wrede, Schweitzer), who deny that Paul made a justification-by-faith-alone distinction central to his own thinking. More recently, scholars, notably E. P. Sanders[40] have further undermined the unfortunate earlier anti-Judaism tendency in Christian scholarship by showing that Second Temple Judaism was not the legalistic scheme Paul is said to have attacked.

More recently, a few scholars, stimulated by Sanders, have emphasized the inconsistencies and outright confusion present in Paul's arguments. Heikki Räisänen[41] and his student Kari Kuula[42] are especially notable at this point. But it is only when Paul's victims and their accusations are brought front and center that the thrust of Paul's argument in the letter to the Galatians attains the necessary sharpened focus. Only then does a *motive* for Paul's inconsistent argumentation and his denigration of Torah become apparent. In fact, Paul does indeed attack Judaism, but Judaism as caricature. Paul's arguments in Galatians are not the sort, which should have become the foundation of any theological system. One might observe that they have not, inasmuch as the letter to the Romans is generally seen as the basis for both Catholic and Reformation understandings of Paul.

The Silencing of Victims as a Motif of Interpretation

Survivors of persecution are often silenced. Indeed, persecution victims often silence themselves.[43] Upon their bodies, they document violence, terror, hypocrisy, weakness and failure. Their very presence is an embarrassment to those who encounter them and a scandal to those who abused and hurt them, and who frequently are in a position to inflict further harm. Silence, thus appears, even to the victim, to be a mode of protection if not of healing. This means that traumatic memories may be allowed to incubate and even strengthen over time, only to be triggered into articulation by a subsequent event. This triggering event can bring vivid memories to greater consciousness and can even cause the victim to relive the trauma.[44] In the case of the supposed persecution victims in Galatia, the arrival in the community of the persecutor could have been a triggering event.

Once given (or perhaps, demanding?) a hearing, victims of persecution are hard to discredit. Suppose the following: by way of a communication from his converts after he had left the area, Paul was confronted by the truthful allegations of his victims. His belletristic reaction was to move quickly past the allegations by way of a truncated and perfunctory admission (Gal 1:13) and focus his rhetorical skills on a defense which emphasized (1) his having been seized by God for a special mission, (2) his freedom from any judgment whatsoever and (3) his own victimization.

In asserting that Paul's pre-literary situation (and therefore his motives in writing the letter) has been generally misinterpreted, this writer invites the reader to consider Paul in his pre-literary consciousness. Look upon Paul as an ambitious, impassioned man, desiring to reassert his influence with people who had moved away from their allegiance to him because of denunciations made against him after he left the area. Consider *why* Paul wrote this letter before trying to understand *what* he wrote.

If the letter is read aloud, one fairly quickly can see that Paul intends to avoid the burden of self-elucidation while discharging the burden of self-defense. He wishes to be pardoned without having to explain his conduct. Paul's propositions (like all self-serving statements) are designed to call attention to themselves, while undermining counter-propositions. This approach is intended to mischaracterize the pre-literary situation. that is, it is intended to win an argument. Specifically, Paul's hope is to garner support by selective assertions about his past relationships and his prior conduct.

Paul's intentional neglect of aspects of his pre-literary situation is replaced in the document by his claim to sovereignty over his own history. Like others before and after him accused of serious misconduct, Paul wishes to control how he is portrayed to people he cares about. He wishes to be seen as a regenerated persecutor, without any responsibilities or consequences for having been a persecutor. Paul therefore distorts the position(s) of those who have denounced him. The skyline of modern Biblical scholarship certainly contains edifices (with varying esthetic and utilitarian features) which insist that Paul in his correspondence misinterpreted the Judaism of his day. "There are no Jewish parallels to [i.e., Paul's] assessment of the law." (Schoeps);[45] Mack[46] characterizes Paul's "treatment of the Torah" as "audacious and self-serving if not contemptuous and dishonest." These conclusions take on even greater pungency if Paul's polemic is considered with his victims in view. With his victims in mind, one senses desperation in Paul.

"You have heard about me" - the Key to the Pre-literary Situation

In Gal 1:13, Paul writes (rather, dictates), "You heard [*ekusate*] about my former life in Judaism, how I persecuted the church of God to the *extreme [oti kath uperbolen]* and tried to destroy it."

If Paul had already made known his past to the recruits in Galatia, there would have been little reason for him further to defend his pre-Christian career now. Therefore, *this statement is key to the pre-literary situation and is taken here as an admission that Paul did not first bring up his past activities as a persecutor.*

The straightforward construction "you heard" (2nd per pl. first aorist active indicative) does not require a source other than Paul. However, Paul's defense already has caused him to distinguish for his readers what he has told them, over against what others have said. Compare Gal 1:8, ("the gospel we did proclaim") 1:11, ("the gospel which was proclaimed by me") and 1:23: ("they heard"). The construction of Gal 1:13, then, indicates that Paul is acknowledging what others have said about him ("you heard") - not reminding his readers of what he himself already had told them.

Concerning his activities as a persecutor of Christian Jews, Lightfoot[47] wants Paul to say "I told you when I was with you." Paul says no such thing. Burton[48] acknowledges Paul's desire for sovereignty over his pre-literary situation and speculates that Paul had already told the Galatians "the story of his pre-Christian life" including an admission of his role as a persecutor. Dunn[49] theorizes that Paul may himself have told his converts of his former life. Or, possibly, that Paul's adversaries ("incoming missionaries") might have "informed" Paul's converts of his "previous way of life" and then tried to use this information "as a weapon against Paul." But Dunn does not consider the implications of this observation: Paul mounted a defense of himself in response to denunciations, not only by his missionary competitors but by his victims.

Martyn[50] states that Paul's adversaries in Galatia "may have made remarks to the Galatians about Paul's pre-Christian activity, accentuating perhaps his persecution of the church." However, like Dunn and other commentators,

Martyn leaves the matter just there, without further inquiry into the fate of Paul's victims or whether Paul had to answer their accusations made within the churches he had established.

Bornkamm[51] thinks Paul discussed his past misconduct "with no bad conscience whatsoever" and "not as a past wrong, whose memory still torments him." But Bornkamm is incurious about the silence and the fate of the victims of this "orthodox Jew." Like other investigators, Bornkamm takes up Paul's theological propositions as a subject of inquiry without considering the apparent absence of a bad conscience as Paul's strategy for dealing with the denunciations of his victims. In this letter, Paul seems to have thought of himself as he explicitly stated elsewhere: "blameless" (Phil 3:6) of any wrongdoing. He responded as he did to his accusers in Galatia not because he was himself distressed about his conduct but because his converts were. Paul expressed a degree of remorse in other circumstances. See I Cor 15:9.

The Rejoinder of the Persecutor: Vilify the Victim

In his dictated prescript (Gal 1:4) Paul declares that the Messiah Jesus "gave himself for *our* sins, so that *we* might be freed from this present evil age." Paul excluded from these solicitous considerations those who were causing him so much difficulty in Galatia. He probably did not ever know or remember their names and speaks of them as rank strangers to him. They are simply dismissed as:

- Gal 1:7: "those who are terrifying you"
- Gal 1:9: "some one"
- Gal 5:7: "whoever"
- Gal 5:10: "whoever he is"
- Gal 6:12: "those who compel you"
- Gal 6:13: "they"

No "different Gospel" – rather, a personal attack

Paul's defense suggests there was in fact no "different gospel," (Gal 1:6), as he himself acknowledges (Gal 1:7). Rather, Paul is reacting to a highly personal criticism of himself. In Galatia, Paul's former victims may well have avoided all contact with him and come forward after he left the area. Their motivation would have been to discredit him by denouncing him to his new recruits. The victims would have identified Paul as a fanatical leader of enforcers (in Judea? Damascus? See discussion *infra*.), who singled out Diaspora Jews for abuse, for proclaiming Messiah Jesus.[52] His victims would have denounced Paul (Saul?) the Persecutor as one and the same Paul the Apostle who had recently arrived to organize assemblies of believers among the Celtic population of the region.

Paul's Integrity Brought into Question

As suggested, Paul needed to defend himself against truthful accusations of his brutal mistreatment of members of a sect in which he now claimed a leading role. This state of affairs would have been confusing, provocative and frightening to Paul's new recruits in Galatia, who may have been told Paul could not have been credentialed by the leaders of the group he had earlier tried to destroy. Even though he clarified that his missionary activity was conducted by agreement with leading Christian Jews in Judea (Gal 2:9), Paul acknowledged that his presence was accidental, the result of illness (Gal 4:13). He has also acknowledged (Gal 1:23) that the Judean churches, rather than sponsor him in some manner, expressed relief that he was no longer on the attack.

With Paul's earlier misconduct as well as his credentials and even his motives brought into question, some of the new converts would have distrusted his sincerity (Gal 1:20). Others may have announced their return to their earlier Celtic religious affiliations (Gal 4:9-10)[53] or (in the case of a few) their intention to return to or identify more closely with Judaism (Gal 5:2).[54] Some probably indicated an interest in becoming Jewish proselytes and submitting to circumcision (4:21).[55] Some may have let it be known they simply wished to have nothing more to do with Paul (Gal 1:6; 4:16; 6:1). These varied reactions have the ring of truth; when a church splinters, even a homogeneous one, and people scatter, they do not all depart in the same direction.[56]

Paul Responds by Characterizing Torah as a Guardian Displaced by an Apocalyptic Event

In light of the denunciations made against him, Paul perceived that he must (1) defend himself against his victims' truthful accusations and (2) try to clarify why the Galatians must not suffer any loss of faith in Messiah Jesus. Facing the quandary, Paul hit upon a line of reasoning which (he believed) offered him both a personal defense and a ground for his converts' continued belief in the Messiah. Consistent with the Gentile mission, he announced that Torah observance had been abrogated *for everyone* by the arrival in history of the Messiah Jesus. But Paul went on to assert that Torah observance was a "yoke of slavery." Paul's employment of the unfortunate[57] Hagar-Sinai metaphor concludes with this very claim (Gal 5:1): "Into freedom, then, Christ has freed *us*. Stand firm, then! And do not allow yourselves again to be placed in a yoke of slavery!" In light of Gal. 2:18 (and discussion *infra*) Paul is suggesting that he could no longer be subjected to judgment for *his* misconduct because *no one* was any longer subject to such judgment, which after all, has been predicated upon a system (Judaism), that functioned, Paul now asserts, as an agent of sin.

In the letter, Paul restates in a variety of ways the principle of impunity from judgment. He offers, for example, the analogy to family relations, with God as father and Messiah Jesus as son. The son shows the way of obedience to the believers, who are themselves, by virtue of the faithfulness of the Messiah-son, accorded adopted status (Gal 4:1-7). Because of the generous behavior of the natural child (who accepts but then transcends enslavement to cosmic forces), the adopted children are acknowledged as having the same status with the natural child. All the children, together, are children of God; all are, together, freed from the control of guardians and managers. The guardians and managers are here described as "rank upon rank of cosmic elements" and as "the law" (Gal 4:3,4).

Paul argues that God undertook the adoption, commissioned the guardians of the minor child (children) and in due time, sent the natural son to liberate the minor children by assuming their lowly status. Paul's point: the arrival of the heir, the natural son, has made possible the entrance into their cosmic inheritance of those who formerly were enslaved to cosmic powers, which included the law. These enslaving powers, first and foremost, religious obligations and practices, are no longer controlling in the lives of the believers.

Despite his imposition of an idiosyncratic cosmic design upon Judaism, Paul would have expected any Jewish readers of his letter to understand Torah as the displaced guardian (Gal 3:17-18). Likewise Paul would have expected non-Jewish believers (a great majority, no doubt, in the churches in Anatolian Celtica) to understand they have been liberated from the requirements of cultic practices commonly observed in their communities, that is from their own "law." (Gal 4:8 f.)

Note how Paul manages to include himself in the freedom manifesto he articulates for the newly converted Gentiles: "*All* are freed from the law--for *we* have been adopted." (Gal 4:5) "Because *you* are children--God sent the Spirit into *our* hearts" (Gal 4:6). Here, Paul implies what he states frequently elsewhere (Gal 2:15-21; 3:10-14, 18-19, 21-25): Paul's past conduct should not cause him to be judged under the now defunct law of the custodial epoch.

The Transitory Purpose of Torah Observance: Regulate Good Conduct and Condemn the Bad

On three occasions in this letter, Paul contrasts the law's condemnation of misconduct with the transcendent status of the believer.

1. To accept condemnation is to question God's grace.

Gal 2: 18-21: *"But if I build up again that [i.e., the system of observances] which has been taken down, I truly am a transgressor! For through the law, I am dead to the law. I have been crucified with Christ! I no longer even live; rather Christ lives in me. Although I live on in the flesh, I live in the faith of the son of God who loved me! And who gave himself for me! I dare not question God's grace! If through the law one can be vindicated, then Christ died for nothing!"*[58]

Dictating - and probably gesticulating dramatically - Paul rejects the idea that he might be subjected to judgment for his past misconduct. Indeed, to permit himself to be judged would recreate the very conditions which could cause him to become "a transgressor." If the point here is that Paul is refusing to permit himself to be judged by the law of the pre-Messiah epoch, we do not then have to decide whether Paul means to imply that the law caused transgressions or was merely the occasion for a sharpened or heightened awareness of transgressions.[59]

2. The purpose of the Law was to restrain misconduct - but only until the arrival of the Messiah.

Gal 3:19: *"Why, then the law? It was added because of transgressions, until the Seed should come concerning whom the promise had been made."*

Paul asks and answers the question: why was the law instituted at all? His answer: The law was appended (as an afterthought?) to the cosmic design in order to regulate transgressions in the historical interim, which ends with the fulfillment of a bequest to Abraham's heirs upon the advent of the Messiah. Paul even specifies the exact period of time in which the law is operative, from 430 years after Abraham until the arrival (that is; until the death, Gal 1:4; 5:11) of the Messiah Jesus (Gal 3:17, 19.)

3. The transgressor must be "restored."

Gal 6:1: *Brothers (and sisters): if any person is discovered in some transgression, those of you who are spiritual restore him with a gentle spirit, watching out for your own selves that you are not tempted as well."*

Paul concludes the letter with admonitions to good behavior and appeals for harmony within the assemblies. In these concluding remarks he employs the same term, transgression (*paraptoma*) that he had applied to himself (Gal 2:18) as well as to the fundamental but temporally limited role of the law (Gal 3:19).

From these three statements, it is apparent the term, "transgressor," ties Paul's central propositions together as his primary defense: The law existed for a time to restrain transgressions (Gal 3:19). But that time has expired and so Paul will not again submit to the law and permit himself to be judged as a transgressor (Gal 2:18). At Gal 6:1 Paul concludes his appeal with one final attempt to win back the good will of his recruits. By speaking of an anonymous "transgressor" he hopes the believers' assemblies in Galatia will accept him as they did once before, restoring him to his (now lost) status as teacher and guide.[60]

Is the Issue Circumcision?

A number of passages in the Galatians letter seem to point towards circumcision as the central dispute. Four passages in particular must be considered if the victim theory is to be maintained. These passages are Gal 2:12; 5:2-6; 5:11; 6:11-13.

Gal 2:12: *"The circumcised" who came from James*

"For before some from James had come, Peter ate with the Gentiles [non-Jewish believers]; however, after they came, he withdrew and held himself apart, fearing the circumcision [the Jewish believers]."

At Gal 2:12, Paul focused his attention on an incident, which becomes the point of departure for the balance of his comments to the Galatian believers. When Peter visited the assembly in Antioch, he ate with all of the believers, Jews and Gentiles alike. However, on the arrival of some believers from Judea, allied with James on the issue of table fellowship, Peter declined to eat with Gentiles on the grounds of ritual impurity. Peter withdrew. His withdrawal caused the other Jewish believers present on this occasion likewise to decline to eat with the Gentiles who were also present. Even Barnabas, Paul's Jewish colleague, held back.

What motivated Peter and even Barnabas to decline communion with non-Jewish believers? Probably, a quest for compromise. Confronted with demands from some arriving Judean believers that ritually observant Jews (the circumcised) and ritually unclean Gentiles (the uncircumcised) be separated at table, Peter, Barnabas and the others may have concluded that, on this occasion-- while there are Jewish visitors unexpectedly present from Judea who are offended--we will agree to their demands and not eat the same food as the Gentile believers.

Paul does not state how the Gentile believers in Antioch reacted. One would think that if they, like Paul, were offended by the Judean withdrawal, Paul might have said so. He does not. [61] In the retelling Paul does not conclude his description of the incident but instead launches an attack on a position he hopes the Galatian believers must support him in: the Messiah assemblies are open to all without any requirement that the adherents be Torah observant.

Gal 5:2-6: *A further attempt by Paul to Define the Issue as a debate not about himself but about a Messianic Manifesto*

Paul presents the issue as one not for or against his credentials and his credibility bur rather as a decision for or against allegiance to the Messiah. At those of his converts disposed to combine adherence to the Messiah and observance of Torah, Paul shouts (Gal 5:1): *"You are freed! It is inconceivable that you would voluntarily turn back from freedom and make yourselves slaves again to the law of the old epoch. I, Paul, will have none of it!"*

Paul is reacting to the effect upon his converts of his victims' denunciations of him to the Celtic churches as a former Jewish extremist and zealot, a persecutor of Messiah adherents, who now is passing himself off as a leader of the movement he tried to crush. To discredit their tormentor of years ago, they have raised questions about Paul's credentials: *Did he tell you the founders of the Messiah Jesus movement continue to observe their Jewish law? Did he tell you whether those founders recognize Paul as a leader of their sect? Did these leaders send Paul here? Or did he just show up on his own? Has he been asking you for money?*

In response, Paul has already admitted that he had not been sent to Anatolian Galatia by the Judean leadership (Gal 2:2). Rather, he had reached a territorial accommodation (Gal 2:9). He also attempted to clarify why funds were needed in Jerusalem and why he was raising them (Gal 2:10) He has also admitted that he "portrayed" (Gal 3:1) Messiah Jesus differently than the portrayal of other adherents (Gal 1:11-12). In response to a likely accusation that he is a brigand, operating without authorization from anyone, Paul reminded the Celts that he appeared among them only after being waylaid by illness (Gal 4:13). He now attempts, repeatedly (Gal 2:18-21; 3:23-25; 4:4-5; 4:8-11), to deflect the personal attacks against him into a debate about ritual observances.

Gal 5:2 "... *if you become circumcised Messiah is of no value to you.*"

Paul directs this comment specifically to those who have responded to the victims' charges by indicating they intend to combine adherence to Messiah Jesus with Torah observance, that is, those "of you who wish to follow the law" (Gal 4:21). This is not the intention of all (Gal 4:10) and so all are not addressed.

Paul asserts that Torah observance by Jews or Gentiles after the advent of the Messiah amounts to a denial of the Messiah. This declaration takes him to an extreme position. The law (Torah) is not simply invalidated by the advent of the Messiah. Rather, *observance of the law invalidates the Messiah*. Paul lays out this proposition in yet one more attempt to remove the ground from under his accusers' efforts to cause his Celtic converts to judge Paul for his past conduct. As he has already stated (Gal 2:18), he will not become an accomplice in an effort to reestablish the authority of the law, and open the door to an assessment of his own past, i.e., permit himself to be judged a transgressor.

Paul may have been pacing, making his points by counting them off on his fingers:

If you accept the symbol of law observance, which is circumcision, remember this: you then have to become fully Torah observant; now if you want to stand before God by Torah observance, you have cut yourselves off from the Messiah; we, on the other hand, confidently expect to stand before God in the spirit sent to us by the

Messiah, because, in Messiah Jesus, law observance means nothing! All that matters now is faith at work, through love!

Gal 5:3: *"All men who submit to circumcision then are obligated to observe the entire law."*

Here we encounter one of the more idiosyncratic of Paul's opinions. Why must any who wish to follow part of the law be condemned if they fail to observe all of it? Paul does not say. Were he asked this question, Paul might respond (Gal 3:19), *If portions of the law were inapplicable, why would these portions have been given?* Paul does not dwell on this difficulty because he believes the Messiah has come and so the whole law has been abrogated. (Gal 2:21b; 3:19) As seen, Paul has supplemented this conviction with apocalyptic ideas about the close of one age and the opening of another. In the new Messiah-dominated epoch, all law, whether Torah or Gentile, is a dead letter (Gal 4:4-5).

Gal:5:6 *"Faith at work through love"*

If Paul, at 5:6, is once again (Gal 1:13) making a confession, he is asking not for forgiveness but for recognition that the two epochs have turned as a door on its hinges. The old standards simply do not apply. If the law-observant epoch has been closed and the new Messiah-controlled epoch has opened, Paul believes he has no need of forgiveness. His mission is to open eyes to the new reality. Neither he nor anyone should be judged by the standards of the old epoch. All that matters is "faith, at work through love." What can this mean? Paul provides few details before closing his letter. He makes his faith-through-love point in order to conclude his comments about the passing away of law observance and the changing of the epochs.

Gal 5:11: "... *for that would remove the scandal of the cross.*"

"*And what about me, sisters and brothers? If I still preached circumcision, why am I still being persecuted?*" This question appears in a particularly intense polemic (Gal 5:7-12) in which each phrase alternates from attack to appeal to attack again. Paul blasts away in utter frustration. When read aloud, it is clear (to this reader, at least) that Paul senses he has lost credibility in Galatia beyond all hope of recovery. Too many of the believers have indicated they no longer have confidence in him. Paul has been abandoned by those whom he himself had organized. He simply cannot believe he has lost ground to people who are complete strangers to his mission.

The "small leaven" (v. 9) may be a reference to the insidious effects the insignificant complaints of the victims are having. However, I think it more likely Paul is referring to his own point of view, expressed in the letter itself. Paul seems to be hoping against hope, suspecting this final appeal is not enough to recover the ground lost. Because of that, he threatens punishment once again--this time nothing less than the holy wrath of the Messiah. No sooner does he issue the threat--against one who already has been a victim--than he catches himself and states that he also is a victim of persecution.

Gal 5:11 suggests that Paul is referring either to his pre-Christian career as a persecutor or to his previous activities as an apostle to Gentiles, who stipulated the necessity of circumcision as did those "from James" (Gal 2:12) – an approach which differed from his present program. Crediting Paul with an evolving perspective and both him and his intended recipients with contextual information no longer available to us about the details of Paul's activities, it simply is not possible to know what circumstance Paul has in mind. Nonetheless, with customary clarity, Dunn[62] has laid out various permutations and concludes, significantly, Paul offers a "*dismissive ad homonym response.*"

If Paul is referring to his life "in Judaism," than he is simply reminding his Celtic converts that he, himself, has suffered persecution, just as his accusers claim to have suffered. On the other hand, Paul may have in mind Jewish hostility engendered by his recruitment of converts to belief in Messiah Jesus. In this case, he is asserting (v. 11) that he has drawn hostility because he has invited *Gentiles* to faith in the executed Messiah. That is, he has not limited his appeals to "circumcision" i.e., to Jews alone, to those who observe Torah. This suggests that Paul met a hostile reaction in or around Diaspora synagogues, where he made a three-fold proclamation *to Gentiles as well as to Jews:* (1) the Messiah has arrival upon the earth; (2) the Messiah was executed; and (3) Jews and Gentiles alike are to enter into the Messianic community, without concern for observances specified by Torah. Stating such convictions as he sought Gentile recruits within earshot of the synagogues of the Diaspora, it is no wonder that he met with violence. Inevitably, if not frequently, he would have encountered a "Saul" who took furious exception to his efforts to combine both Gentiles and Jews in the sect of the Messiah.

Whatever description of events this statement suggests, Paul is attempting to win sympathy from his recent converts. He is also seen to be urgently engaged in a polemic whose objective is to deflect denunciations by some of the victims of his own persecution, who wish to subject Paul to condemnation as a persecutor of Messiah Jesus adherents.

Why would Law Observance remove "the scandal of the cross?"

Paul introduces (5:11b) an eccentric interpretation of the consequences of law observance, which amounts to yet another novel line of argument: the *lawful* putting to death (execution) of the Messiah is scandalous. As the instrument of a scandal of cosmic proportions, the law has forfeited even its interim authority. Were Paul then to concede the reinstatement of the law, he, himself, would remove this ignominy and thereby would himself render the crucifixion empty of significance. Paul here repeats a point he had made somewhat differently in Gal 2:18-21: if he were to submit again to the chastening function of the law, then Christ died for nothing. There also seems to be an echo of Gal 3:10-14, wherein Paul expresses the peculiar notion that the Messiah became "cursed" either by God or by the Law by hanging on a tree. [63]

The announcement of the invalidation of the law upon the advent of the Messiah is within the horizon of opinions available to messianic Judaism of this period. As suggested, this announcement, combined with an invitation to enlist Gentiles in the messianic movement would likely be sufficient to provoke persecution. However, by declaring that the law itself has put the Messiah to death Paul is taking an anachronistic position no Jew could maintain.[64] Once taking this position, it is not surprising, then, that Paul would defend it by asserting that he will not remove the cruciform scandal. As suggested, this understanding of 5:11 is coherent whether Paul has in mind his former *preaching* of law observance (circumcision) as a member of the sect of the Pharisees or as *preaching* a Torah-free gospel to God-fearing Gentiles in or near the synagogues.

There is no basis for Paul's adoption of the extreme views expressed in Galatians except his enraged urgency to deflect accusations directed at him personally: he is a lawless, menacing freebooter and a dangerous proponent of violence. Paul's response to such charges is to assert there is nothing to be gained by looking backward, because, with the Messiah, everything has changed; the temporary dispensation which accorded a role to the law has been abandoned, torn down (Gal 2:18), as it were. Paul now says: *were I to advocate the requirements of the old epoch ("preach circumcision"), I would remove the infamy now attached to the law by the crucifixion ("the scandal of the cross")*. Removal of this scandal would make pointless the Messiah's faithfulness (Gal 2:16) unto death (Gal 2:21).

Gal 6:11-13: Paul now claims victimhood for himself.

Having reached the conclusion of this angry, defensive letter, Paul takes the pen from his secretary and scratches out one more castigation of the opposition. *"Look with what large letters I write to you in my own hand! As many as want to make a favorable impression in the flesh, these same ones compel you to become circumcised -- but only so they will not be persecuted on account of the cross of Christ! Those who are circumcised--they do not even observe the law -- but they want you to be circumcised so they can boast in your flesh!"* (Gal 6:11-13)

His final blast is typically personal. His accusers are motivated by fear as well as pride. On the pretext of avoiding more problems for themselves, they care for nothing except impressively to make demands. In fact, they want only to demean the believers.

"They compel you . . .". Paul is using the identical verb he used to describe Peter's actions in Antioch, when Peter (Cephas) withdrew from the table of those believers who were not circumcised. (Gal 2:14: ". . . you compel Gentiles to adopt Judaism"). Of course, Peter was not in a position to compel any particular conduct; he could only withdraw if he did not approve, which is what he did.[65] As E. P. Sanders has stated, " . . . the charge that Peter was 'forcing the Gentiles to live like Jews' [. . .] goes beyond the story as [Paul] tells it."[66] By asserting they possess the intent to "compel" the Galatians to become circumcised, Paul is distorting the motives of his adversaries, just as he did in Gal 2.

More than likely, no one has tried to compel circumcision of the Celts, most of whom, but not all (Gal 5:2), would have been disgusted and offended at this humiliating and painful procedure. Paul is emphasizing the Jewish initiatory rite of circumcision in order to try one more time to win back his estranged recruits, who have been influenced against him.

Paul's accusers probably went no further than to point out that Paul, a Jew himself, no longer was Torah observant, and that this failing, combined with his earlier persecution of the very group he now purported to lead, casts doubt upon his reliability as a guide in important matters. Responding to this kind of personal attack, Paul suggests his critics are merely afraid of a renewal of persecution directed at themselves. His comments are but a sarcastic rebuttal of the denunciations of his victims. In Gal 6, Paul's arguments against circumcision are directed at undermining the credibility of the victims by charging them with cowardice.

Paul's arguments, here, as elsewhere in Galatians, fit the range of stratagems employed by the Persecutor to deflect the credible accusations of the Victim. These stratagems have been well described by Herman[67] as follows:

> "In order to escape accountability for his crimes, the perpetrator does everything in his power to promote forgetting. Secrecy and silence are the perpetrator's first line of defense. If secrecy fails, the perpetrator attacks the credibility of his victim. If he cannot silence her absolutely, he tries to make sure that no one listens. To this end he marshals an impressive array of arguments, from the most blatant denial to the most sophisticated and elegant rationalization. After every atrocity one can expect to hear the same predictable apologies: it never happened; the victim lies; the victim exaggerates; the victim brought it upon herself; and in any case, it is time to forget the past and move on."

Paul concludes by taking up the theme of his own victimhood: *"As for the rest of it, let no one attempt to trouble me for I am carrying the signs of the Lord Jesus upon my body!" (Gal 6:17)* Paul looks to marks upon his body as his final argument against his victims: *"Don't bother me about that. I have myself become one of the persecuted."*(Gal 6:17). This reference is not to the spirit but to the flesh and is ironic, coming from Paul. It probably would have accomplished no more than to remind the believers of the denunciations of Paul's accusers. If Paul lost these little Celtic assemblies, who gathered to worship a Jewish Messiah, he lost them not to another Gospel oriented to law observance. He lost them to his own history.

CONCLUSION

This attempt to recover the pre-literary situation in Anatolian Celtica is an effort to account for the particularity of an occasional letter and thus to address certain ambiguities present in the preserved text of the letter. These peculiar features including the following:

- Paul is enraged and defensive
- In Galatia Paul is not opposing a coherent theological position, rather
- Paul is confronting personal criticisms and attacks
- Paul is ambivalent how best to answer his critics who appear to be (former?) adherents themselves, whom he does not identify
- Paul's attitude towards his converts/addressees alternates between fury and solicitousness
- Paul's assertion that observance of the law causes sin, is without precedent in Judaism[68]
- Paul's expressed more moderate views in Romans

The recognition that Paul's adversaries in Galatia are his former victims – not competitors - does much to clarify these ambiguities. Paul, the accused, Paul the persecutor, is expected by his recruits to give an account of his conduct. In consequence, he presents a self-defense, which includes a variety of styles of argument. These statements, which include metaphor (Gal 4:1-7) and allegory (Gal 4:22-5:1) are not consistent with each other. All of the rhetoric is employed in the service of a larger exculpatory argument, whose foundation is an assertion of impunity. None of the rhetorical techniques employed, the metaphorical and allegorical flourishes in particular, should be subjected to the imposition of logic thinking or the search for sequential, linked propositions, otherwise foreign to Paul in this letter. In Galatians, there exists no warrant to stretch Paul's contentions into a theological system.

Recognizing Paul's victim as his accusers in Galatians permits us to dispense with the contrivance of a category of variously described adversaries, evidence for whose existence is not otherwise to be found: "teachers" (Martyn), "judaisers" (Burton and Bultmann), missionary-agitators (Kuula), heretical Gentile converts (Munck), or Gentile converts to Judaism and/or their Jewish mentors (Nanos),or provocateurs (Esler). The existence of such opponents in Anatolian Celtica is based on no more than inference, which is contradicted by lack of evidence for a law-observant, circumcision-requiring mission directed by Jews at Gentiles. On the other hand, Paul's victims existed beyond any doubt (Gal 1:13). Isn't it only plausible, then, to speculate that the victims surfaced [69] to denounce Paul in Galatia and possibly elsewhere?

Paul asserts in this dictation that Torah observance is a positive menace to the standing of the Messiah-community before God. This extreme claim is highly idiosyncratic and is not required by any known factors in the pre-literary situation. This claim is most clearly explained by self-defensiveness and is certainly not to be seen as part of the proclamation of the pre-Paul gentile mission. A very much temporized denigration of Torah may be found in Paul's subsequent letter to the Romans. It is persuasive (to this writer) that Paul adopted a volatile anti-nomian position as but an additional argument to throw up against the credible and effective personal attacks[70] of people he had abused prior to his conversion.[71]

However, a victim theory must come to terms with at least three issues: (1) Paul's motives as a persecutor; (2) the locale where the persecution took place and (3) the dating of the letter to the Galatian churches.

What about Paul's motivation as a persecutor? If Paul's victims - Jewish adherents of Jesus as Messiah - had announced the abrogation of Torah observance *for Gentiles* and *for Jews,* they might have suffered at the hands of Jewish enforcers such as Paul announced himself to have been. Acting on instructions from temple (Jerusalem) or synagogue (Damascus) authorities, these enforcers could have concluded that a Messianic sect, which permitted Gentile membership without observance of Torah, was a threat of defilement to the Jewish community as a whole. This would mean that the pre-Paul Gentile mission of inclusion in common meals without purification requirements was the activity, which stimulated Paul to violent reaction. It may be worth noting, once again, that Paul, responding to his accusers in Galatia, went beyond the claim of the inapplicability of Torah observance to Gentile and Jewish messiah-adherents, by asserting the death-dealing aspects of "the law."[72] It may also be the case, as Räisänen[73] speculates, that Paul was scandalized at the announcement of a Messiah executed by crucifixion, that is, hanged on a "tree" (Gal 3:13; see Deut 21:23).

Where did Paul's persecution of the believers take place? If Paul's activities were confined to the Diaspora from start to finish, we may hypothesize that persecuted Christian Jews moved from, say Damascus, to central Anatolia, there to denounce Paul to newly minted believers. If the motive for Paul's persecution of Jewish believers was their inclusion of non-observant Gentiles in a bogus Messianic sect, a Diaspora setting makes sense. However, Gal. 1:22-23 suggests that we should leave open the possibility that Paul's persecution of Messiah-believing Jews took place in Jerusalem. In his own words (Gal 1:22), Paul was not known personally to the Judean believers. But Paul immediately states (Gal 1:23) Judean believers had felt themselves targeted by him ("the one who persecuted *us*") but nevertheless (v.24) gave thanks for Paul subsequent change of heart. The statement of thanksgiving would of course be more credible if it came from someone other than the persecutor. In any case, to remove Paul from any connection with persecution in Jerusalem because he was personally unknown by Messiah adherents in Judea requires the acceptance of Gal 1:22 as a statement of fact but the rejection of Gal 1:23 because it is not factual but rhetorical.[74]

A third question has to do with the dating of the letter. A late date for the composition of Galatians would undermine the victim theory, as Paul, in subsequent letters remarks (I Cor 15:9; Phil 3:6) about his persecution of believers and qualifies (Ro 2:12-8:4) his anti-Torah position as stated in Galatians. An early date for a letter intended to answer charges that Paul is an unfit and untrustworthy guide provides a particular context, which was not repeated in Philipi or in Rome. On the grounds of the history of collections for the Jerusalem believers, Martyn[75] has demonstrated that the letter is most likely an early composition: after I Thessalonians but before all of the other undisputed letters. For a discussion of the relative weight to be given to Acts, see Esler[76] who also opts for an early date.

Paul, a devout but volatile Jew of the Diaspora, devised an idiosyncratic reading of the Hebrew Scriptures in defense of his persecution of other Jews. These, his victims, were Diaspora Jews who had frequented one or another of the Messiah Jesus assemblies, probably in Jerusalem, possibly in Damascus.[77] Some of the victims, surviving Paul's persecution of them, either relocated or returned to their homes in Anatolian Celtica, whereupon they denounced Paul to his new converts.

In his defensive letter to the Galatian assemblies, Paul endeavored to redefine the issue of his prior conduct as a persecutor and in this way deflect his victims' accusations. In short, he asserted that their denunciations of him were not relevant to the Messianic age. Although he may have failed to win back his proselytes in Galatia with these arguments, Paul did succeed in silencing his victims throughout the history of the church down to the present.

His letter of self-defense was preserved; their accusations and denunciations were not.

NOTES:

1. Lightfoot, **Galatians** (1865, Zondervan, 1957) page 242.
2. J.L. Martyn, **Galatians** (Doubleday, 1997) page 282; J.D.G. Dunn, **The Epistle to the Galatians** (Hendrickson, 1993) page 151.
3. M. Luther, **Commentary on Galatians** (Revell, 1988) page 123; although Calvin believed the Galatians of Anatolia were probably "Belgae" and not Celts, he looks to Pliny in support of his conclusion that "the Galatians inhabited that part of Asia named after them [. . .]." **New Testament Commentaries**, (Eerdmans 1965), vol 11, v.
4. W. Meeks, **The First Urban Christians** (Yale 1983) page 42.
5. Please see Lightfoot, page 242; see also T. Powell, **The Celts**, Thames and Hudson (1980) at 20; one of the few modern commentators to examine the ancient literary evidence is P. Esler, **Galatians** (Routledge, 1998) at 29-36.
6. Please see Dunn, pages 9-11.
7. Please see Martyn, pages 117-126; see also Martyn, **Theological Issues in the Letters of Paul** (Abington, pp 7-24 (1997)
8. T. Aquinas, **Saint Paul's Epistle to the Galatians** (Larcher 1966) page 160.
9. Please see Luther, page 47.
10. E. Burton, **Galatians** (T&T Clark 1921, 1968) page liv; see also R. Bultmann ("Judaizers" in Galatia), **Existence and Faith**, Shubert Ogden, ed. (Meridian, 1960, page 116).
11. Please see Lightfoot, page 27.
12. Please see Luther, pages 47, 341.
13. J. Munck, **Paul and the Salvation of Mankind** (Knox, 1959) page 134.
14. H. Räisänen, **Paul and the Law** (Fortress, 1986) 258, 264.

15. M. D. Nanos, **The Irony of Galatians: Paul's Letter in First-Century Context** (Fortress, 2002) page 6. Nanos' suggestion that Paul in Galatians has adopted "ironic rebuke" as the rhetorical stratagem seems to have been anticipated by Dahl, as Nanos generously acknowledges, citing (41, 338) an unpublished paper Dahl presented in 1973. It is notable, however, that where Dahl discovered "disappointment" and "reproach" in Paul's letter, Nanos detects (34) irony alone.
16. See Esler, page 51.
17. E. C. Gruen, **Diaspora: Jews Amidst Greeks and Romans** (Harvard, 2002, page 47).
18. Id.
19. Scot McKnight, **A Light to the Gentiles: Jewish Missionary Activity in the Second Temple Period**, (Augsburg Fortress, 1991, pages 116-117)
20. The absence in Acts of any reference to a Jewish mission to win proselytes "corresponds to the historical setting." Irina Levinskaya, **The Book of Acts in its First Century Diaspora Setting** (Eerdmans, 1996) at 49.
21. See McKnight, generally and the discussion in Levinskaya, Id., 52 f.
22. Please see Lightfoot, page 71.
23. W. Wrede, **Paul**, 1908, Reprinted by Wipf and Stock, ND, page 123. Albert Schweitzer declined to see "justification" as the central emphasis of Paul, opting for "being-in-Christ" as the "prime enigma" which "gives the clue to the whole." **The Mysticism of Paul the Apostle** (1931, Seabury, 1968) page 3.
24. Esler, at 153. Esler, interestingly, concludes that righteousness was a "reactive teaching" in Paul, not the core of his theology. There are contrary views. See especially E. Käsemann, **New Testament Questions of Today** (SCM, 1969, pp. 168-183). See also J.C. Beker, **Paul The Apostle**, Fortress (1980), at 23-58, who rightly stresses the importance of contingent circumstances in assessing Paul's letters.
25. Please see Burton, page liv.

26. Nanos, page 318.
27. Id. at 126.
28. E. Käsemann, **New Testament Questions of Today** (Fortress 1969), page 14.
29. Martyn, pages 37, 101, 252, 276.
30. R. Bultmann, **Theology of the New Testament** (Scribner's Sons, 1951), vol 1, page 224.
31. John Macquarrie, **Principles of Christian Theology** (Scribners, 1966), 105-10, 166-70.
32. A helpful summary of the philosophical side of these developments is found in Jean Grondin, **Introduction to Philosophical Hermeneutics** (Yale, 1994).
33. B. Mack, **Rhetoric and the New Testament** (Fortress 1990) 66-73.
34. H.D. Betz, **Galatians** (Fortress, 1979).
35. See Nanos, page 34. Martyn, at 117, 146-48, sees Paul's use of rhetorical technique as a "reproaching" of his original presentation when in Galatia.
36. Esler, pages 15-20, 58-92, esp. 19, 61.
37. Kari Kuula, **The Law, the Covenant and God's Plan** (Finnish Exegetical Society 1999), page 31.
38. Mack, page 68.
39. "Paul portrayed the Law itself as an enslaving tyrant, thus expressing a view of the Law foreign to all strains of Jewish and (first century) Jewish-Christian thought known to us." Martyn, **Theological issues in the Letters of Paul**, Abington (1997), at 42.
40. **Paul and Palestinian Judaism**, (Fortress, 1987).
41. Räisänen, page 14.
42. Kuula, **The Law, the Covenant and God's Plan** (Finnish Exegetical Society 1999), generally.
43. My views have been influenced by my experience as an attorney in the United States, representing persons fleeing persecution.
44. Judith L. Herman, **Trauma and Recovery**, (Basic Books, 1992). Pp. 8, 37, 87.
45. See H. Schoeps, **Paul, The Theology of the Apostle in the Light of Jewish Religious History** (Westminster,

1961) at 174. Schoeps also states (175): "The Pauline inference that the law, which could not prevent universal sinfulness, and on the basis of which no man [sic] could be justified by his works, is a law unto death [citations omitted] is one which no Jew could draw." See the discussion in Esler, pages 145-159. Schoeps' interpretation of Paul and the Torah has not received adequate attention in the commentaries. Betz (xiii) judges Schoeps' book as possibly "the best book on Paul" in the 20th century, but then dismisses Schoeps as "the modern recreation of the criticism of the ancient Pauline opposition." (Id.) Räisänen, in his preface, states "most Christian replies to Schoeps are clearly beside the point."

46. Mack, page 72.
47. Lightfoot, page 81.
48. Burton, page 44.
49. Dunn, page 55.
50. Martyn, page153.
51. Bornkamm, G., **Paul** (Harper and Row, 1969) pages 14-15.
52. The Book of Acts, (7:54-8:1) places Paul in Jerusalem, when the believer Stephen was murdered by a mob of stone throwers. Acts implies that the Judean believers escaped persecution, while believing Jews from the Diaspora were hounded out of town. This persecution, according to Acts 8:1, touched everyone "except the Apostles." Acts, therefore, offers support for the conclusion that official (i.e. lawful) persecution was directed not at Judean believers, but at Hellenistic Jewish pilgrims. Acts arises from a later pre-literary situation but this fact does not require Acts to be deemed inherently unreliable as a guide to occurrences in Paul's career. As John Knox observed years ago, "some of the Tendenz to be found in [Luke's] work almost certainly belonged in the first instance to the sources he employed." ("Acts and the Pauline Letter Corpus," **Studies in Luke-Acts** (Fortress, 1966, 1980, eds. Keck and Martyn) 282.
53. Suggestions that Paul, at 4:8-10, is confronting a movement among the Galatians towards Christian-Jewish

(Martyn) or simply Jewish (Dunn) Torah observance and not a return to aspects of Celtic or other local religious beliefs are not persuasive. Martyn, **Galatians**, at 415 sees in these verses a Christian-Jewish discernment of "holy times" arrived at "by watching the movement of the stars." Dunn, finds the reference to observance of Jewish years "puzzling" (228) but nevertheless thinks (226) "the idiom" of turning back "is very Jewish." The reference, however (v. 9), is to turning back "again" which cannot apply to Judaism if Gentiles are predominantly the addressees. Paul is confronting a reversion to previous local religious practice on the part of some of the Celtic converts. See Burton, at 231.

54. Paul, in the towns of Anatolian Celtica, probably recruited Jews as well as Celts and addressed them all in his letter. Martyn concludes (**Galatians**, page 16) otherwise, arguing there could not have been Jews among these converts, because there were none in Anatolian Celtica by the First Century CE. However, the complete absence of Jews in either Paul's newly founded churches or in Anatolian Celtica is unlikely. Martyn does not comment on an Augustinian decree erected in Ancyra, ordering the protection of *Ioudaioi*. Josephus, **Jewish Antiquities** Book 16, Chapter 6 (**The Works of Flavius Josephus**, Coats & Co., ND, trans. By W. Whiston, 486), cited by Esler, at 31 as **Jewish Antiquities** 16, 165.

55. Räisänen, in a significant observation (page 261, footnote 163) states, "The Galatians seem to be exceptional in their willingness to accept circumcision." There is no evidence cited which might have pointed to such openness. Suppose the Galatians were not exceptionally open to being circumcised? Doesn't this suggest Paul's polemic in the letter may have been directed against circumcision primarily (1) to elicit support for him and also (2) to change the subject away from the denunciations made against him?

56. Some helpful attention has been paid to group theory as an analytical matrix to be applied to Galatians. See especially

Esler. Group theory may be more helpful if applied to the idea that Paul's converts were influenced against him by his victims, rather than by competing missionaries.

57. Paul employs the analogy to direct a further threat against defenseless adversaries, as Hagar and her son are depicted: "For what does the written word say: 'Cast out the slave woman and her son for the son of the slave shall not inherit with the son of the free woman'." Gal 4:30. Martyn (**Theological Issues**, at 201), identifies the targets of Paul's call for a Celtic Anatolian persecution, not as Jews per se, but rather "representatives of the Gentile mission." But this distinction does not soften or lessen the implicit brutality of Paul's expulsion instructions to his Galatian converts, pursuant to the Hagar-Sinai analogy.

58. Gal 3:2, 5.

59. See Kuula (pages 134-167), who stresses that Paul denied a divine origin to Torah and asserted that the law causes transgressions.

60. The Latin copyists, whose work is to be found in the Vulgate, do not hesitate to assign varied meanings to Paul's words, thus obscuring his self-defensive purpose. At 2:18, the transgressor is a "praevicator" but not at 3:19, where transgressions are "transgressiones", at 6:1 transgression is "delicto." See **Novum Tesatamentum Graece et Latine**, eds. Nestle-Aland (Deutche Bibelgesellshaft (1984) and Libreria Editrice Vaticana (1986).

61. Martyn, (**Theological Issues**, page 31), correctly describes this event as a "political defeat" for Paul, engineered by the "False Brothers" (Gal 2:1-10). The Damascus encounter was clearly a defeat for Paul. However, I suggest the "false brothers" were not leaders in Judea but rather former believers (therefore, "false brothers") who no longer participated in the life of the Jerusalem gathering of believers; they were allowed in ("slipped in") specifically to denounce Paul as their erstwhile persecutor. Paul recast their censure as a threat to the freedom of the Galatians (!) and conceded "nothing" to them.

62. Dunn at 278-80.
63. See P. Fredriksen, **From Jesus to Christ** (Yale, 2000) at 147.
64. Martyn is right to detect (**Galatians**, pages 37-45) between Galatians and Romans a softening of Paul's statements concerning the law. Martyn considers this softening (1) little more than a clarification (2) due to the presence of Jews in the church in Rome but not in the churches in Galatia. But in Romans, Paul moves decidedly away from his assertions in Galatians (3:19, 23, 4:4-5, 5:18) that the Law is "adversarial, not to say, quasi-demonic." See P.W. Meyer, "The Worm at the Core of the Apple," **Studies in Paul and John, In Honor of J. Louis Martyn** (Abington, eds. Fortna and Gaventa, 1990) at 82. For our present purpose, which is to consider the implications of the presence in Galatia of Paul's victims, it may be enough to say, with Mayer, Paul "changed since Galatians." It may be more precise, still, to say that the two situations simply were different.
65. Paul employs the same word in his triumphant announcement (Gal 2:3) of Titus' entrance into the assembly in Jerusalem without being "compelled" to submit to circumcision.
66. E.P. Sanders, "Jewish Association with Gentiles and Galatians 2:11-14," **Studies in Paul and John, In Honor of J. Louis Martyn** (Abington, eds. Fortna and Gaventa, 1990) at 187.
67. Herman, page 41. See Note 44.
68. "Through the pressure of events he was lead to search for arguments for a global rejection of the law," as Räisänen (page 261) correctly observes. But Räisänen's conclusion (pages 261, 258, 264) that Paul was lead to this "liberal" result because of his intuitive "conscious thinking" which opposed "selectivity" and thus opened the door to "restorers" of Torah observance is unpersuasive.
69. In a forthcoming commentary on Galatians, I will try to demonstrate that the victims surfaced in Jerusalem, in the persons Paul characterized as "false brothers" (Gal 2:4).

70. "It may be that had it not been for these conflicts Paul's stated view of the law would have been a good deal different." Räisänen, (page 256).
71. Esler (pages 69-75) suggests it was a common expedient, in the highly competitive environment of the Greco-Roman world to engage in ad hominem attacks--especially upon critics one did not like or know well. Paul seems to have incorporated this tactic in his letter.
72. As stated, I have concluded Paul adopted in this letter an extreme position against observance of Torah. There are assertions in Galatians that arguably run to a contrary position. But is this the case? These modifying statements include Paul's announcements of love as the mode of fulfilling the whole law (Gal 5:14) and of the existence of "the law of Christ" (Gal 6:2). I take these statements to be exhortations and not a retreat from Paul's bold anti-Torah position. The same is true (following Mack, page 69) of Gal 1:9, which Käsemann interprets as part of the supposed "holy law" of the apostle, who approaches his communities as a "law giver" and who, on this occasion, Käsemann suggests, announces a death sentence against "the guilty." See Käsemann, **New Testament Questions of Today** (Fortress, 1969) 75, 71. One wonders how Käsemann's Paul, would have expected his Celtic converts to carry out the "death sentence."
73. Räisänen, page 249.
74. *Contra* Räisänen (235). Despite his undue concern to harmonize Paul and Acts, see R. Riesner, **Paul's Early Period**, (Eerdmans, 1998) at 72, for some plausible arguments.
75. Martyn, **Galatians,** pages 19-20.
76. Esler, pages 32-36.
77. E. Haenchen stated half a century ago that Paul, then living in Damascus, "persecuted the local Hellenistic community through the means at his disposal in the local synagogue." See "The Book of Acts as Source Material for the History of Early Christianity," **Studies in Luke-Acts** (Fortress, 1966. 1980, eds. Keck and Martyn) page 264. Following

Haenchen, is it possible that Paul's victims and antagonists in Galatia included Gentiles, who would have been motivated to denounce him in no less strident terms than would have been Hellenized Jews?

PAUL ... PREACHER OR EVANGELIST ?

Evangelistic activity in Paul's day certainly included communication by word, just as it does in our day; but it also included much more. Thus, as the translator comes to Paul's letters, it is important to be aware of Paul's strategies and tactics. Fundamentally, Paul was an organizer, a founder of house churches. He felt called by God to spread the Gospel as he understood it (Rom 1.1-7, 9.3, I Cor 2.2-5, 2 Cor 10 & I 1, Phil 1.19-24). His daily concern was the state of each little congregation he had established (2 Cor 11.28).

Details about Paul's activities as a missionary (organizer) are scattered throughout his letters. But one of the best pictures of his work is found in Romans 15. In verses 18-20 we see that Paul's goal was to organize communities of believers of all races. His objective was to win a response by any means: word and deed, signs and wonders. His strategy was to work in an orderly way from Jerusalem around the Mediterranean coastline to the Adriatic Sea and to focus his labors in new territories not yet entered by other missionaries or missionary teams. In verses 23-24 we have the remarkable picture of a man in his mid-fifties, after at least 20 years of constant travel, struggle and personal risk - 20 years of hard evangelistic activity - making plans for the next phase of his work.

Paul describes his missionary activities by the verb *euangelizo*. This rare Greek verb is not easy to translate. The noun *euangelion* means "good news" to those who receive it and "a reward for good news" to the person who brings it. However, the verb is much harder to deal with. English does not have a verb which is derived from the noun "Gospel", so we cannot simply say, "I gospel to you" or "the Gospel which was gospeled". Translators have searched for alternatives and have usually chosen to translate *euangelizo* by some form of the English verb "preach."

"Preach", however, is normally limited to verbal activity and implies the delivery of a sermon, usually in the context of worship. Very few translators or New Testament scholars today would consider Paul a "preacher" in the modern sense of this term. Therefore, in translating *euangelizo,* we need to select a word or construct a phrase which conveys the dynamic quality as well as the variety that evangelistic activity had for Paul. The words in italics are my suggestions for translations of *euangelizo* in the following texts. These texts are selected from among the 18 occasions when Paul uses this verb, in his letters to the Romans, the Galatians and the Corinthians.

Gal 1.8-9 *"But if even we ourselves or an angel from heaven* **should present the Gospel** *in a manner contrary to the way* **we presented it** *to you, let him be cursed! As we said before, so now I say again, if any person* **presents the Gospel** *to you differently than how you received it, that person is damned!"*

Paul is not involved in an argument among "preachers" about how to "preach". What is at stake is the identity of the new Christian communities in the province of Galatia, who have been influenced to forsake the unconditional way of relating to each other which Paul *showed* them himself earlier. We might even wish to translate *euangelizo* as "portray" or "live" the Gospel, here.

Gal 1.11 *"I want you to know that the* **Gospel which was disclosed by me** *is not from human beings."*

This play on words ("the Gospel which I gospeled") might also be translated "the Gospel which I embodied in your midst". Paul thought of himself as somehow physically expressing the Crucified Messiah (Gal 3.1, 6.7). And he was received in Galatia as Christ himself (Gal 4.14). It is clear here as elsewhere in Galatians that *euangelizo* refers not simply to preaching but to the total impact of Paul's presence.

Gal 1.23 *"They only heard, 'He who once persecuted us now **is spreading** the faith he tried to destroy.'"*

For Paul, activity on behalf of the Gospel is just as aggressive as activity against the Gospel. Evangelism is hard work (I Cor 15.10) which involves the establishing or planting of Christian communities. The connotations of "preaching" simply do not convey the qualities of engagement and activism which evangelistic labor had for Paul. This is especially clear in Galatians which contains 7 of the 18 occasions when Paul uses the term, *euangelizo*. These chapters reflect conflict and bitter disagreement over fundamentals. Paul is addressing himself not to preachers and other specialists in the churches. He is addressing ordinary people, who have been summoned through his witness to reverse their values and live a life of service and solidarity with Christ (Rom 8.16-17).

I Cor 1.17 *"For Christ did not send me to baptize but to **live the Gospel**-not in eloquent speech, lest the Cross of Christ be made empty."*

Paul draws a distinction here between Gospel presentation and the power of words. He felt called to demonstrate the power and authority of the Cross through "weakness" and "fear and trembling" rather than by means of profound, moving address (I Cor 2.1-5).

I Cor 9.16, 18 *"Yet even if I am able to **live the Gospel**, this is nothing I should boast about. Necessity is laid upon me. Woe to me if I do not live the Gospel! [. . .] What then is my reward? By living the Gospel as I do, I make the Gospel free of charge, not even claiming my rights in the Gospel."*

It was being said in Corinth that Paul was unworthy of material support. He answers that his lifestyle and his missionary practice (9.1-7) entitle him to support even when he doesn't claim it. Paul is certainly not talking about being paid to preach.

I Cor 15. 1-2 *"Now I would remind you, brothers and sisters, of the Gospel* **which I presented** *to you-in what terms* **I presented the Gospel** *to you-which you received, in which you stand, by which you are saved-if you continue to hold it."*

Paul used *euangelizo* to encompass all of his strategies as a missionary-organizer. This included his practice of recounting the so called *facts* or the historical content of the Gospel, in particular the record of resurrection appearances. As he writes or perhaps dictates this letter, he wishes to make clear for himself and for his readers that he now is talking about the traditions he had received and passed on. This is why he repeats himself: ". . . the Gospel which I presented--4that is to say) in what terms I presented the Gospel." (The RSV hides this distinction by skipping over the first appearance of *euangelizo* in this passage.)

2 Cor 10.16 *". . . in order* **to establish the Gospel** *in lands beyond you . . ."*

As we have seen, Paul's goal was to organize new communities of Christians. He expects to move into areas beyond the province of Achaia, areas untouched by other missionaries, and establish churches there.

Rom 10.15 *"And how can they preach unless they are sent? As it is written, 'How welcome are the feet of those who* **bring good news!***'"*

Just as in I Corinthians, we find here a close connection between preaching and other kinds of evangelistic activity. However, this means that the role of the preacher is expanded. Gospel activity is not narrowed down to mean only the use of words. Paul is talking about the prophets, who conveyed "good news" in dramatic and creative fashion. In many cases they attempted even to embody the message they brought. Paul says also that the word about Christ is also the "event" *(rimatos)* of Christ (verse 17), which must be *lived*.

Rom 15.18-20 *"For I will not dare to speak of anything except that which Christ has done through me to win a response from all peoples - by word and deed, through the power of signs and wonders, through the power of the Spirit-so that from Jerusalem as far around as Illyricum the Gospel of Christ has been established - making it my goal* **to live the Gospel** *not where Christ is named lest I build on another's foundation."*

We have already seen how helpful this passage is in demonstrating the variety and range of Paul's missionary labors and strategies, which include word, deeds, signs and wonders. Paul did indeed "preach Jesus" but he did so in his lifestyle and in his work as a missionary-organizer. It is interesting to note in this passage the fondness of translators for the term "preach," which is used here to translate another Greek word, *peplerokenai,* which literally means, "made full".

CONCLUSION

Paul's use of *euangelizo* does not support the repeated use of "preach" in translation. For good or ill, "preach" has taken on in English clerical and technical senses. A translation of *euangelizo* in any language should not be limited to a term, which implies only communication by word. Also, in many churches the preaching ministry is limited to ordained persons. But Paul is not writing to preachers in his letters; a word or phrase must be used which will address *each* believer and Bible reader in his or her own situation. Paul challenged *all* his readers to imitate him (I Cor 4.16, 11. 1, Phil 4.5). He was not thinking only of those who are called to specialized ministries in the church, but saw evangelism as an activity for each Christian.

PAUL, THE ORGANIZER

The quality of intimacy and urgency, which comes through in the letters of Paul has probably given many Christians through the ages a sensed bond with Paul as a fellow struggler. Others, while intuiting a closeness with Paul, beyond that, may dismiss him as an obscure, difficult or irrelevant thinker. While New Testament scholarship of course pays a good deal of attention to Paul, Christian activists outside the New Testament "guild" betray little interest in these scholarly pursuits. Perhaps this gap can be bridged by attempting to identify Paul's strategies as an organizer of house churches. Recognizing this activity as central to Paul's life, we will be able to see that Paul was very much an activist.

Paul's strategies and techniques have been neglected by scholars and missiologists alike. The tendency has been to move away from specifics about Paul's activities and focus instead on his thought.[1] Paul's missionary practices, we are told, are not as important as the principles behind them.[2] Paul's letters indicate that he was consumed by the idea of planting churches and spreading his understanding of the gospel. So it is curious that so little interest has been taken in Paul's day-to-day activities as a missionary-organizer and in his specific plans, objectives and goals. A good deal of material on these subjects is to be found in his letters but frequently this material is dealt with only incidentally by scholars who come upon it while in pursuit of some other objectives.[3]

We know that Paul was occupied daily with concern about the welfare of the little congregations he had established (II Co 11:28). Although these concerns gave impetus to much of his thought, it is said that Paul's real significance for Christians today is his impact as a, theologian.[4] While this view is fundamentally correct, this may be due in part to the neglect of Paul's life-style and work in favor of a scholarly interest in his thought.

The starting point of any theological inquiry will likely determine the end point. As Robert McAfee Brown said:

"Where do we begin our theological inquiry? Christian history offers many answers to this question. A favorite one starts with nature and concludes from an examination of order or beauty or causality that there must be a God. Another starts with the givenness of a set of claims made by an infallible book or an infallible church and works from that self-authenticating revelation to a world on which the revelation sheds light. A third starts with the inherently rational nature of the human mind and concludes that a universe out of which such rationality could evolve must itself be the creation of a Supreme Mind. Liberation theology has a different starting point. Its starting point is the poor, the 'marginalized,' those about whom the rest of society could not care less." (1978:60).

If one assumes, at the beginning of the quest, that Paul dealt mainly with ideas and themes such as justification by faith, grace and law, or freedom and obedience, then one can go on forever refining and sifting one's own ideas - and never actually do anything. However, what if Paul's main idea is not an idea at all but action? It seems to me that we need to deal with the challenge Paul issued to his readers: "Imitate me!" (I Co 4:16, 11:1; Phil 4:9). How are we to imitate Paul unless we take a good look at how he spent his time? My own starting point is the conviction that one must move from study into action to make proper use of the insights gained from scholarship.

Paul asserts that Christians play a role in reclaiming God's creation, which has fallen into corruption (Ro 8:21-22). As affluent Christians we have a special responsibility to take this task seriously, since we possess so much of the technological and economic tools of the world. Existing church structures do not seem able to address the grave ethical problem of affluence. Books with revolutionary titles, literary and homiletic exhortations and church resolutions that contain words like peace, justice, and hunger are not very impressive or important apart from risky and sacrificial deeds to back up all the words. It was not in the study but in the middle of a road where Paul had his life turned around. By not giving proper emphasis to Paul's organizing techniques, we subtly refashion Paul in the image of the objective intellectual and scholar who is engaged with the world primarily by "doing" theology, i.e., reflecting and writing. This is true however much we talk about "reading" Paul in his own context because so little weight is given to what was most important to Paul day in and day out: organizing people. A closer look at Paul's strategies seems in order.

Paul Was the Leader of a Team of Missionary-Organizers

Paul referred to his team members by name: "Silvanus, Timothy and I" (II Co 1: 19). We know that Paul had a number of other co-workers - Titus, Barnabas, Sosthenes, Phoebe, Junia and others. Both the number and the identity of his co-workers varied from time to time and place to place. Paul's co-workers were central to his work. And Titus, for example, apparently was more effective than Paul with regard to raising funds in Achaia for the poor Christians in Jerusalem (II Co 12:18).

Further evidence of the importance of Paul's co-workers is that all the undisputed letters are from Paul and his partners in the missionary enterprise. (See the introductions to I and II Corinthians, Galatians, I Thessalonians, Philemon, Philippians.) The single exception is Romans, which is more of a treatise than a letter occasioned by inquiries or events in a specific congregation. Galatians excepted, it appears that Paul wrote letters on behalf of Silvanus, Timothy, Sosthenes and others who had labored with him and who were with him when he wrote a particular letter.

Paul and His Team of Co-Workers Practiced a Division of Labor

Paul did not baptize as a part of his regular routine (I Co 1: 14-17), which means that someone else did. Paul's responsibility, once the team had established themselves in' a particular location, was to give instruction on various subjects, including the nature and order of worship (I Co 12:8-1 1), the role of the Spirit-filled person (I Co 14), and the meaning of Jesus' Resurrection (I Co 15). Paul also passed on the traditions he himself had received (I Th 4:1-2; I Co 10:1-3, 15:3-7; Phil 2:5-1 1). At the time, when Paul wrote his letters, he and his co-workers organized primarily (thought not exclusively) among Gentiles (1 Th 2:14; Ro 15:26-27, 16:4). A good deal of instruction in the Hebrew Scriptures must have taken place for Paul to quote so extensively from these writings. It seems likely that Paul conducted this instruction and that he was the chief teacher-trainer on the missionary team.

The Team Followed a Fixed Itinerary

Paul indicates that he worked in an orderly way "from Jerusalem as far around as Illyricum" (Ro 15:19) - around the Mediterranean coastline to the Adriatic. The team stayed for months at a time in one province or area (I Co 16:5-8), but once the gospel had been "established" (not "preached", Ro 15:19) and house churches had been founded, Paul felt there was no longer "room" (Ro 15:23) in these regions. In Romans 15, we see the remarkable picture of a man in his mid-50s, after at least 20 years of struggle, hardship and itinerancy, making plans for the next phase of his worldwide strategy, a journey to Rome and the West. Despite all the risks, Paul the disciplined, intentional strategist could say in truth, "I do not run aimlessly; I do not box as one beating the air!" (I Co 9:26).

Churches Were Organized Through Demonstrations of Power

Paul's initial activities on arriving in a new community were probably centered in the marketplace, where he worked a good deal of time to support himself. There was something unusual or peculiar about Paul which he took advantage of in his organizing efforts. Paul may have used his handicap, whatever it was, to draw attention to himself. This does not mean that he willingly accepted his physical limitation in some fatalistic or neurotic sense; rather he was stuck with his handicap, saw it as a means for divine power to be seen in his life and turned it to advantage (II Co 12:7-9). It was due to some "physical infirmity" (Gal 4:13) that he successfully reached people in Galatia; his initial contact with people in Corinth was through "weakness" and "fear and trembling" (I Co 2:3). Paul felt that in his own person Jesus could be seen as "crucified" (Gal 3: 1), and the marks of the crucified Jesus were actually visible on Paul's body (Gal 6:17). Time and again, Paul would parlay hardship and suffering into an appeal to form and remain loyal to congregation struggling to survive.

Customs Threatening House Churches Were Opposed

Paul refused to permit the circumcision of Titus (Gal 2:3) and he would not let his newly-won converts participate in the cultic celebrations of other deities (I Co 10: 14), engage in sexual conduct which threatened the peace of the congregation (I Co 5:1-3) or take one another to court (I Co 6:1-8). Activities and practice should be "tested" to see whether they build up or destroy (I Th 5:21; I Co 12:26; Ro 14:19-20).

Paul was Flexible and Pragmatic About Cultural Differences

Having followed Jewish cultic and dietary laws rigorously, Paul now declared them no longer binding on "the Israel of God" (Gal 6:16). The focused, disciplined organizer knew the difference between what was important and what was not. Paul could eat non-kosher food with Gentiles (Gal 2:12), yet in Judea where such regulations were of great importance to Christians who continued to worship in the temple at Jerusalem, Paul followed at least some of the customs of Judaism (Ac 21:26). His religious practices were variable because of the task which lay before him: "I have become all things to all people so that I might save some by all (whatever) means" (I Co 9:22).[5]

National and religious customs are all of relative importance (I Co 7:17-24; Ro 14), but they are not more important than the peace of the congregation. Christians are not to pass judgment on one another regarding such matters. Indifferent about what days one observes, what one is to eat or what one's social status is, Paul was concerned with belonging to the Lord's community (Ro 14:7-8), in whom there is freedom (II Co 3:17).

Several of Paul's Co-Workers Were Women

Phoebe, Prisca, Mary and Junia are all mentioned in Romans 16. Several popular translations (RSV, JB, NEB - with a footnote) refer to Junia as Junias. Could this be because Paul calls her an "outstanding apostle" (Ro 16:7)? W. Bauer's comment is illuminating: "The possibility from a purely lexical point of view, that this is a woman's name [. . .] is probably ruled out by the context" (1967:381).[6]

"Apostle" Implies Organizer

Simply transliterating *apostolos* into English has created a distance between us and Paul. The word *apostolos* means "messenger" or "envoy." Paul uses the term to designate himself and others who carry forward the missionary task: establishing congregations of believers throughout the world. In his polemical attempts to assert his authority as an *apostolos,* Paul points to "signs, wonders and mighty works" (II Co 12:12). He argues that the very existence of the house church is "proof" of his *apostole* - his commission - and his success as an organizer (I Co 9: 1-2). He has demonstrated his authority by having worked harder than other missionary-organizers (I Co 15: 10).

Paul does not base his apostleship on having been a witness to the resurrection of Jesus. Nor does he imply that he is the only apostle (I Co 9:5; II Co 1 1:5 9 12:1 1). There were other witnesses to the Resurrection who were not apostles (I Co 15:5-7) and likewise there were apostles who have no apparent claim to a resurrection appearance (Ro 16:7). Paul knows that he is an apostle because he has worked hard (I Co 15: 10) and has been successful. I Cor 9:2 virtually says, *You yourselves cannot deny that I organized successfully among you.* Paul was an apostle because he felt himself to be sent and because he actually did what he had been sent to do: establish churches.[7]

Preaching Versus Evangelism

Paul defines his activities by using the verb *euangelizomai*. Although few New Testament scholars would argue that Paul was a "preacher" in the modern sense of that term, over and over *euangelizomai* is translated "preach". The noun, *euangelion*, gospel, means "the good news" to those who hear it or "a reward for good news" to the one who brings it. But the verb, *euangelizomai*, is more difficult to translate.

Transliteration would give us, "I gospel to you" and "the gospel was gospeled." Though most English versions render this verb by some form of the verb "preach," it would seem *preach* is not a functionally equivalent translation for *euangelizomai*. This verb is not limited by grammar, etymology or its use outside the New Testament in a way, which requires that it mean the spoken word or oral address – to the exclusion of other actions.

The Greek verb *kerusso* "to herald" or "proclaim aloud" is used by Paul 15 times in the undisputed letters (he uses *euangelizomai* 18 times). *Kerusso* implies an oral presentation, but *euangelizomai* does not (Bauer 1967:317-318; 432). This means, there is no reason to assume in Paul's usage that "the bringing of Good News" or the presentation or delivery of the gospel is limited to the spoken word.

"Preach" in contemporary English implies the delivery of a sermon. A check of virtually any dictionary will confirm this. "Preach" does not convey the range of meanings that *euangelizomai* had for Paul. More varied, dynamic translations are called for. Some suggested substitutions for "preach" in translating **euangelizomai** would include:

Galatians 1:8-9

But if even we ourselves or an angel from heaven **should present the gospel** *in a manner contrary to the way we presented it to you, let him be cursed! As we said before, so now I say again, if any person* **presents the gospel** *to you differently than how you received it, that person is damned!*

Paul is not involved in an argument among "preachers" about how to preach. What is at stake is the identity of the new Christian communities in Galatia who have been influenced to forsake the unconditional way of relating to each other which Paul *showed* them earlier.

Galatians 1:11

*I want you to know that the gospel **which was disclosed** by me is not from human beings . . .*

This is a play on words - "the Gospel which I gospeled" (Robertson 1931:277). In the context of this letter, one might even say, "the Gospel which I embodied in your midst," since Paul thought of himself as somehow physically expressing the crucified Messiah (Gal 3:1, 6:17). Certainly the term "preach" does not convey the depth of Paul's meaning here.

Galatians 1:16

*. . . revealed his son to me so that I **might proclaim** him to all peoples . . .*

Evangelistic activity certainly includes oral proclamation and so "preach" might fit this text - as long as it is clear that Paul is not thinking only of the spoken word about Jesus. Paul's gospel proclamation included his missionary strategies and goals, his life-style, all his day-to-day activities. *Perhaps "that I might live him before all peoples"* would be the best translation in this context.

It is worth noting in passing that *ethne* ought not be limited to "Gentiles" in Paul's letters, nor should it be assumed that Paul never organized among Jews prior to the Apostolic Council (Gal 2, Ac 15). Paul himself refers to missionary activity in Judea (Ro 15: 19), and Acts records frequent visits to synagogues, which may reflect Paul's actual practice at an early point in his career. The key issue in Galatians is not that Paul would exclude Jews, as opposed to *ethne;* rather that Paul insisted *everyone* be included in the new communities he was establishing under the authority of the crucified Messiah.

Galatians 1:23

"They only heard, 'He who once persecuted us now is spreading the faith he tried to destroy.'"

Gospel activity is just as aggressive for Paul as persecution. (Perhaps by the time he dictated this letter, Paul has modified his overtly violent and coercive stratagems.) Nevertheless, evangelism is hard work (I Co 15:10), which involves the establishing (Ro 15:19) or planting (I Co 3:6) of Christian communities.[8] The modern connotations of "preaching" simply do not convey the thoroughly dynamic quality of Paul's activity.

Galatians 4:13

*You know that it was through a physical ailment that **I presented the gospel** to you the first time.*

It is not clear whether Paul's physical condition was an incidental factor, which accounted for his staying in Galatia or whether it was the instrument Paul used to establish his work there. But it is clear that preaching "because of a bodily ailment" (RSV) can be understood only if preaching refers to the total impact of Paul's presence among the Galatians. Paul was received by them as Christ himself (4:14).

I Corinthians 1:17

*For Christ did not send me to baptize but **to live the gospel** not in eloquent speech, lest the Cross of Christ be made empty.*

Paul distinguished between gospel presentation and oratory or philosophical presentations. He felt himself called to demonstrate the power and authority of the Cross through "weakness", "fear and trembling" rather than profound, moving address (I Co 2:1-5).

I Corinthians 9:16, 18

*Yet even if I am able **to live the gospel** this is nothing I should boast about. Necessity is laid upon me. Woe to me if I **do not live the gospel**! . . . What then is my reward? By **living the gospel as I do**, I make the gospel free of charge, not even claiming my rights in the gospel.*

It was being said in Corinth that Paul was not worthy of material support. He answers that his life-style and his missionary practice (I Cor 9:1-7) entitle him to support - even if he doesn't claim it. Paul is certainly not talking about being paid to preach.

I Corinthians 15:1-2

*Now I would remind you, brothers and sisters, of the **gospel which I presented** to you - in what terms I **presented the gospel** to you - which you received, in which you stand, by which you are saved - if you continue to hold on to it.*

Paul goes on to spell out the key, traditional elements of his preaching. Since Paul uses *euangelizomai* to encompass all his activity as a missionary-organizer, the historical content of the gospel is not what immediately suggests itself to Paul. Since "gospeling" means *a way of life* to Paul, he must clarify for himself and his readers exactly what he is talking about. And so he repeats himself: "the gospel which I presented - [that is to say] in what terms I presented the gospel."

II Corinthians 10:16

*. . . in order **to establish the gospel** in lands beyond you.*

Paul's goal is to organize new communities of Christians. He expects to move into areas beyond the province of Achaia, areas untouched by other missionaries, and establish churches there.

II Corinthians 11:7

*Did I commit a sin by living poorly myself so that your status might be raised - since I **lived the gospel** of God without charge to you?*

Paul was being compared unfavorably to other missionaries who apparently were good preachers (II Cor 11:5-6) and received support in Achaia for their labors. In response, he calls attention to his life-style as justification for being worthy of financial support and (then confusedly) his refusal to accept it. The issues are clouded by using the term "Preach".[9]

Romans 1:15

*And so I am eager **to live** among you in **the gospel**.*

Paul here is addressing an established congregation, which he intends to visit so that they might mutually strengthen and encourage one another (1: 12). "Preach the gospel to you" (RSV, GNB) has revivalist connotations which are foreign to this context. "Bring the Good News" (IB) is descriptive of Paul's prospective activities not in Rome but in new territories where churches do not yet exist.

Romans 10:15

*And how can they preach unless they are sent? As it is written, "How welcome are the feet of those who **bring good news!**"*

Here, as in I Corinthians 15, we find a close connection between preaching and evangelistic activity. But this means that the role of the preacher is expanded - not that "gospeling" is narrowed down to only oral proclamation. Paul is talking about the prophets who conveyed the "good news" in dramatic and creative fashion, in many cases attempting even to embody the message they brought. The word about Christ is also the "event" *(rematos)* of Christ (v. 17), which must be *lived*.

Romans 15:18-20

*For I will not dare to speak of anything except that which Christ has done through me to win a response from all peoples - by word and deed, through the power of signs and wonders, through the power of the Spirit - so that from Jerusalem as far around as Illyricum the gospel of Christ **has been established** - making it my goal to live the gospel not where Christ is named lest I build on another's foundation.*

Since Paul's evangelistic activity included word and deed, signs and wonders, he talks here about the range of his missionary labors and strategies - working in an orderly way; organizing communities of believers of any and all races *(ethne)* in new territories not yet entered by other missionary teams. All these objectives are summarized in the phrase **establish the gospel**.

Evangelistic activity for Paul involved concrete, specific actions in obedience to the crucified Messiah. Evangelism means action in service and not simply preaching.[10] This seems especially clear in Galatians 1 and

2, which contain 7 of the 18 occasions when Paul uses the term *euangelizomai*. The tenor of these chapters reflects conflict and bitter disagreement over fundamentals. Paul addressed himself in Galatians and elsewhere not (exclusively) to preachers and other church specialists, but to ordinary people who had been summoned through his witness to reverse their values and live a life of service in obedience to the crucified Christ (Ro 8:16-17).

CONCLUSIONS

Paul did indeed "preach Jesus", but he did so in his life-style and in his work as a missionary-organizer and activist. If we could recover something of the intensity and challenge of Paul's faith we might in turn rehabilitate that fine word, Evangelism. The calling of the evangelist is not to revivalism or quietism but to action. Evangelism is an activity for all Christians - not just "preachers."

All who are engaged in the Christian missionary enterprise, who are trying to live with Paul under the sign of the Cross (II Co 5), may get practical help from seeing Paul as an organizer who focused on concrete ways to get this job done.[11] He was the leader of a disciplined team of workers who traveled together and probably lived in community as they moved from place to place. Their first priority was to organize - to plant (I Co 3:6) - house churches, nurture them for a time and then move on. In the midst of these shared labors they lived a vulnerable, risk-filled life. This context, in which Paul worked out his ideas, needs to be kept in mind as his ideas are interpreted and applied to other situations in other times and places.

The successors of Paul today are the theologian-activists, Christian thinkers-and-doers who call the affluent church to live truly in the service of the crucified, who is present in the persons of the struggling poor, the marginalized and oppressed, the sinned against, those erased from history, non persons (I Co 1: 26-28).[12] These theologian-activists demonstrate in our day the meaning of evangelism as Paul, the passionate, intense activist did so long ago. His challenge, "Imitate me!" invites us all to become evangelists, adopt a life-style of vulnerability, to build community with one another in the conviction that all of life and death itself are under the authority of the crucified Christ.

NOTES

1. R. Bultmann wrote in 1930, "an essential part of Paul's accomplishment consists in his having joined the Christian communities into a firm unity" (*Existence & Faith:* 119). As far as I know, Bultmann never develops this insight; instead he always deals with Paul as a theologian and as a major influence in the history of ideas. In his *Theology* Bultmann gives less than three pages to Paul's "historical position" and even here treats Paul's thought and not his missionary practice (1951:187-189). John Koenig's approach to Paul is helpful as he wishes to take "a close look at the way in which Paul uses eschatological mysteries to help his readers receive, understand and practice God's *charismata.*" To Koenig, Paul insists that the proper understanding and use of charismatic gifts leads "to mutual service in the community - in other words, to hard work" and Paul is preparing his churches for "the long haul" (1978:167-173). Here we have a successful effort to bridge the centuries as we catch a glimpse of Paul the missionary-organizer and strategist.
2. "The person who contends that the missionary *methods* of the apostle Paul are normative for today is not handling aright the Word of God. Only the principles upon which his methods are based are of abiding validity." (Glasser 1979:103).
3. The conclusions of scholars regarding Paul's techniques and strategies are rather offhand and very diverse. Dibelius and Kümmel say that "it was not he who organized and managed the church" (1975:68). A. Schweitzer concludes that Paul "is only a thinker, not a tactician" (1968:156). J. Munck suggests that Paul's motives are important but not his actual practices (1977:65). In John Knox' view, Paul is "in all but name, the bishop of a large diocese, [. . .] increasingly occupied with the problems of the pastor and the

administrator" (1955:103). E. Käsemann refers to Paul as "a lone wolf and an alien" (1974a:71). G. Bornkamm in his book on Paul offers no thorough examination of Paul's missionary strategies but distinguishes between his "work" and the "outer circumstances of his life" (1971:xxviii).

4. Wayne A. Meeks poses the question, "Was Paul a theologian, an activist or a mystic?" He answers that "there can be no question but that he would have to be called the missionary [activist?] first and foremost. But if we ask about the impact of his career on the lasting forms of Christianity, it is equally clear that it was his thought that was important" (1972:441).

5. G. Bornkamm deals with Paul's missionary techniques as principles rather than as concrete actions; he writes of this passage, "Paul intends the statements to characterize a practical stance of solidarity with various groups, rather than to describe several ways of adjusting his preaching in terms of culture and language and environments" (1966:202). One wonders how "practical" Paul's stance could be without attention paid to such factors as language and culture. For Bornkamm the issues Paul addressed assume the character of an academic debate.

6. Bauer would rule out the possibility that Paul is here speaking of female co-workers. This limitation points to a theological position, which does not admit the possibility that some women missionary-organizers worked independently of Paul or on an equal footing with him. Elizabeth Schüssler Fiorenza has addressed this question as well as the question of Paul's regulations concerning women in I Corinthians 14:34-35 (1978:153-166). In light of the activities of a number of women as founders of house churches, Schüssler Fiorenza finds Paul's instructions (women, specifically wives, should remain silent during worship; they should ask their husbands at home if they have

anything to say) "preposterous". She thinks many Corinthian Christians would have thought so too. It is interesting that she judges Paul's instructions to be based on tactical and strategic considerations: "in the final analysis, however, not theological reasons but the concern for decency and order determine Paul's regulation" (*Ibid*: 16 1).

7. C. K. Barrett makes a distinction between Paul the apostle *of Christ* and others who are apostles *of the churches* (I Co 8:23). But it is not at all certain that Paul set himself apart from his co-workers and other apostles in this way. We know there were Jewish-Christian missionaries at work before Paul and that he embraces them and their labors (Ro 16:7). For Paul an apostle is one who is called and sent into mission (1972:34-81).

8. Raymond Fung has recently given us a refreshing picture of this kind of contemporary church planting and community building, ". . . in the context of trying to share the gospel with the poor, in the context of participating in their struggles for dignity and justice, such as helping them to understand their rights as workers" and "as human beings in front of locked factory gates, in open law courts and in the side chambers of lawmakers, in the open space of protest rallies or within the confines of cement cubicle homes when workers strategize with us and sometimes read the Bible and pray . . . . The Gospel must not only call on people to repent of their sins; it must call on them to resist the forces which sin against them. . . . A community of the sinned-against struggling against forces of sin is an evangelizing context. It is in a community of struggle that evangelism takes place" (1980:230).

9. Paul himself may have clouded the issues by not accepting support from those he organized into house churches. This refusal may have confused some who

were asked by Paul to give money for the poor Christians in Judea. One can imagine them saying, "First he says he is independent and wants no money from us, then he asks for money." Perhaps Titus accepted material support and was therefore a better fund raiser than Paul (II Co 12:18).
10. E. Käsemann says, "Jesus called disciples and did not open a school of perfect theology or of its adepts. Grace that is not active is illusion; only discipleship in our everyday life can justify our dogmatics in the face of the world" (I 974b:60).
11. J. L. Martyn argues that for Paul, the opposite of "according to the flesh" is not "according to the Spirit" but rather "according to the Cross. . . . There is only one point at which the epistemological question can be legitimately posed: the death/resurrection of Christ and the daily death/life of the disciple" (1967:285, 287). Our examination of Paul's missionary practices and strategies would indicate that this was the truth of Paul's own life.
12. Some of the most compelling theological writing today [1981] is that of Wayne C. Hartmire of the National Farm Worker Ministry. See especially the quarterly NFWM newsletter. NOTE: *current (2007) address: National Farm Worker Ministry, 438 N. Skinker, St. Louis, MO 63130. 314 726 6470 - www.nfwm.org*

REFERENCES CITED

Barrett, C. K. **The Signs of an Apostle**, Philadelphia: Fortress Press (1972)

Bauer, W., **A Greek-English Lexicon of the New Testament and Other Early Christian Literature**, W. F. Arndt and F. W. Gingrich, trans. and rev. Cambridge and Chicago (1967)

Bornkamm, G., "The Missionary Stance of Paul in I Corinthians and in Acts" in **Studies in Luke-Acts**, Leander Keck and J. Louis Martyn, eds. Nashville and New York: Abingdon Press (1966)

_____, **Paul**, D. M. K. Stalker, trans. New York and Evanston: Harper and Row (1971)

Brown, Robert McAfee, **Theology in a New Key**, Philadelphia: Westminster Press (1978)

Bultmann, R., **Theology of the New Testament** vol. I Kendrick Grobel, trans. New York: Charles Scribner's Sons (1951)

_____, **Existence and Faith**, Shubert Ogden, trans. New York: Living Age Books (1960)

Dibelius and Kümmel, **Paul**, Frank Clarke, trans. Philadelphia: Westminster Press (1975)

Fung, Raymond, "Evangelism and the Struggle for Dignity" *Christianity and Crisis* (August 18, 1980)

Glasser, Arthur F. "Reconciliation Between Ecumenical and Evangelical Theologies and Theologians of Mission" *Missionalia,* November (1979)

Käsemann, E., **Perspectives on Paul**, Margaret Kohl, trans. Philadelphia: Fortress Press (1974)

_____, **Jesus Means Freedom**, Frank Clarke, trans. Philadelphia: Fortress Press (1974)

Knox, John, **Chapters in a Life of Paul**, New York and Nashville: Abingdon Press (1955)

Koenig, John, "From Faith to Ministry: Paul as Interpreter of Charismatic Gifts" *Union Seminary Quarterly Review* Spring and Summer (1978)

Martyn, J. L., "Epistemology at the Turn of the Ages, 2 Cor. 5:16" **Christian History. and Interpretation**, W. R. Farmer et al., eds. Cambridge (1967)

Meeks, Wayne A., "The Christian Proteus" in **The Writings of St. Paul**, Wayne Meeks, ed. New York: Norton (1972)

Munck, J., **Paul and the Salvation of Mankind**, Frank Clarke, trans. Atlanta: John Knox Press (1977)

Robertson, A. T., **Word Pictures in the New Testament**, Nashville: Sunday School Board of the Southern Baptist Convention (1931)

Schüssler Fiorenza, Elizabeth, "Women in the Pre-Pauline and Pauline Churches" (*Union Seminary Quarterly Review 1978)*

Schweitzer, A., **The Mysticism of Paul the Apostle**, New York: Seabury Press (1968) (trans., William Montgomery)

PRAYER OF COLUMBUS

All my emprises have been filed with Thee,

My speculations, plans, begun and carried out in thoughts of Thee,

Sailing the deep, or journeying the land for Thee;

Intentions, purports, aspirations mine, leaving results to Thee . . .

My hands, my limbs grow nerveless,

My brain feels rack'd, bewilder'd,

Let the old timbers part I will not part,

I will cling fast to Thee, O God, though the waves buffet me, Thee, Thee at least I know.

Walt Whitman

Autumn Rivulets
Leaves of Grass

ST PAUL - PREACHER, EVANGELIST OR ORGANIZER?

Paul's letters indicate that he was consumed by the need to plant house churches and spread his own understanding of the gospel. We know that he was occupied daily with concern for the welfare of the little congregations he had established (II Cor 11:28). These concerns gave impetus to much of his thought. Thus, it is curious that so little scholarly interest has been taken in Paul's day-to-day activities as a missionary-organizer. The conclusions regarding Paul's techniques and strategies are diverse. For example, M. Dibelius and W. Kümmel say: "it was not he who organized and managed the church." A. Schweitzer suggests that Paul "is only a thinker and not a tactician." J. Munck concludes that Paul's motives are important but not his actual practices as a missionary. In John Knox's view, Paul is "in all but name, the bishop of a large diocese," while E. Käsemann thinks of him as "a lone wolf and an alien."[1]

NT scholarship has uncovered much material in Paul's letters, which relates to his specific plans and objectives, but the normal approach has been to focus on his thought and pay very little attention to his activities. The assumption is that Paul's *thought* is what is important and not *how he actually spent his time.*

Paul defines his activities by using the word *euangelizomai* which appears eighteen times in Paul's undisputed letters (Gal 1:8a, 8b, 9, 11, 16, 23, 4:13, 1 Cor 1:17, 9:16a, 16b, 18, 15:1, 2, II Cor 10:16, 11:7, Rom 1:15, 10:15 and 15:20). Although few NT scholars would say that Paul was a *preacher* in the modern sense of the term, it is remarkable how uniformly *euangelizomai* is translated *preach* by several influential translations. The RSV has *preach* consistently except at I Cor 1: 15, where in effect it is omitted, being conflated with *in what terms I preached to you the gospel* (15:2). JB uses *preach*, apart from II Cor 10:16 (*carrying the gospel*) and Rom 1:15 and 10:15 (*bring the Good News*). GNB offers an alternative translation only in I Cor 1:7 (*tell the Good News*), Rom 10:15 (*bring good news*), and Rom 15:20 (*proclaim the Good News*). The NEB has the greatest number of alternatives: *proclaim* in Gal 1:16 and I Cor 1:17, *bring the Gospel* at Gal 4:13 and Rom 15:20, and *carry the Gospel* in II Cor 10:16, *declare the Gospel* in Rom 1:15, and in the Isaiah quotation of Rom 10:15: *messenger of good news*.

It is doubtful whether the overused *preach* gives us a functionally equivalent translation of *euangelizomai, to gospel*. The noun *euangelion* means *gospel* or *good news* to those who hear it and *reward for good news* to the one who brings it. But the verb *euangelizomai* is difficult to translate. We cannot simply say *I gospel to you*, or *the gospel which was gospelled*. Alternative, more meaningful phrases have to be looked for.

There is a Greek verb, which properly means *preach*. Paul uses this verb, *kerusso*, fifteen times in the undisputed letters. Now *kerusso* literally means *to herald* or *proclaim aloud*. Thus, while *kerusso* implies an oral communication *euangelizomai* does not.[2] In Paul's usage, *the bringing of Good News* or the presentation or delivery of the gospel is not limited to the spoken word. *Preach* in contemporary English is invested with churchly overtones and implies the delivery of a sermon. My point is that *preach*, is not only the English equivalent of an entirely different word (*kerusso*) - preach does not convey the range of meanings that *euangelizomai* had for Paul. More varied, dynamic translations are called for. The italicized words in the following texts are my suggestions for translations of *euangelizomai* as alternatives to preach.

Gal 1:8-9

But if even we ourselves or an angel from heaven **should present the gospel** *in a manner contrary to the way* **we presented it** *to you, let him be cursed! As we said before, so now I say again, if any person* **presents**

the gospel *to you differently than how you received it, that person is damned!*

Paul is not involved in an argument among *preachers* about how to *preach*. What is at stake is the identity of the new Christian communities in Galatia, who have been influenced to forsake the unconditional way of relating to each other which Paul *showed* them earlier. (NOTE: Since 1981, My thinking has been modified. I now believe Paul was being undermined in Galatia by his earlier victims, who denounced him to his converts. (See pp 53-92, above.)

Gal 1:11

I want you to know that the gospel which ***was disclosed*** *by me is not from human beings.*

This is a play on words - *the gospel which I gospelled*. In the context of this letter, one might even say, *the gospel which I embodied in your midst*, since Paul thought of himself as somehow physically expressing the crucified Messiah (3:1, 6:17). Certainly the term preach does not convey the depth of Paul's meaning here.

Gal 1:16

. . . revealed his son to me so that I might ***proclaim*** *him to all peoples . . .*

Evangelistic activity certainly includes oral proclamation and so *preach* might fit this text - as long as it is clear that Paul is not thinking only of the spoken word *about* Jesus. Paul's gospel proclamation included his missionary strategies and goals, his lifestyle, all of his day-to-day activities. Perhaps *that I might live him before all peoples* would be the best translation in this context.

It is worth noting in passing that *ethne* ought not to be limited to Gentiles in Paul's letters. It should not be assumed that Paul never organized among his own countrymen - prior to the (so-called) Apostolic Council (Gal 2, Acts 15). Paul himself refers to missionary activity in Judaea (Rom 15:19). Acts records frequent visits to synagogues, which may reflect Paul's actual practice at an early point in his career. The key issue in Galatians is not that Paul would exclude Jews, as opposed to *ethne*. Rather, Paul insisted that *everyone* be included in the new communities, which he was establishing under the authority of a crucified Messiah. (See NOTE at Gal 1:8-9.)

Gal 1:23

*They only heard, 'He who once persecuted us now is **spreading** the faith he tried to destroy'.*

Evangelism is hard work (I Cor 15:10) which involves the establishing (Rom 15:19) or planting (I Cor 3:6) of Christian communities. Contemporary connotations of *preaching* simply do not convey the thoroughly dynamic quality of Paul's activity.

Gal 4:13

*You know that it was through a physical ailment that **I presented the gospel** to you the first time.*

It is not clear whether Paul's physical condition was an incidental factor which accounted for his staying in Galatia or whether it was the instrument which Paul used to establish his work there. But it is clear that *preaching because of a bodily ailment* (RSV) is an adequate translation only if *preaching* is taken to refer to the total impact of Paul's presence among the Galatians. Paul was received by them as Christ himself (4:14).

I Cor 1:17

*For Christ did not send me to baptize but **to live the gospel** - not in eloquent speech, lest the cross of Christ be made empty.*

Paul draws a distinction between gospel presentation and oratory or philosophical argument. Paul felt called to *demonstrate* the power and authority of the cross through *weakness* and *fear and trembling* rather than profound, moving address (I Cor 2:1-5).

I Cor 9:16, 18

*Yet even if I am able to live the gospel, this is nothing I should boast about. Necessity is laid upon me. Woe to me if **I do not live the gospel!** [. . .] What then is my reward? **By living the gospel as I do**, I make the gospel free of charge, not even claiming my rights in the gospel.*

It is being said in Corinth that Paul is not worthy of material support. He answers that his lifestyle and his missionary practice (9:1f) entitle him to support - even if he doesn't claim it. Paul is certainly not talking about being paid to *preach*.

I Cor 15:2

Now I would remind you, brothers and sisters, of the gospel which I presented to you - in what terms I presented the gospel to you - which you received, in which you stand, by which you are saved -if you continue to hold on to it.

Paul goes on to spell out the key, traditional elements of his preaching. But by using *euangelizomai*, which encompasses all of his activity as a missionary-organizer, the historical content of the gospel - that which can be articulated in words - is not what immediately suggests itself to Paul. Since *gospelling* means *a way of life* to Paul, he must try to clarify for himself and his readers exactly what he is talking about. And so he repeats himself: *the gospel which I presented - (that is to say) in what terms I presented the gospel.*

II Cor 10:16

. . . in order **to establish the gospel** *in lands beyond you*

Paul's goal is to organize new communities of Christians. He expects to move into areas beyond the province of Achaia, areas untouched by other missionaries, and establish churches there.

II Cor 11:7

Did I commit a sin by living poorly myself so that your status might be raised - since I **lived the gospel** *of God without charge to you?*

Paul is being compared unfavorably to other missionaries who apparently were good preachers (II Cor 11:5-6) and received support in Achaia for their labors. Paul calls attention to his life-style both as justification for his insistence that he is entitled to financial support and yet his refusal to accept any such support. The issues are clouded by using the term *preach*.

Rom 1:15

And so I am eager **to live** *among you* **in the gospel**.

Paul is addressing an established congregation, which he intends to visit. He wishes to visit them that both he and they might mutually strengthen and encourage one another (1: 12). *Preach the Gospel to you* (RSV, GNB) has revivalist connotations which appear to be foreign to this context. *Bring the Good News* (JB) is descriptive of Paul's activities in new territories areas where churches do not already exist. This would not apply to the church at Rome.

Rom 10:5

And how can they preach unless they are sent? As it is written, 'How welcome are the feet of those who **bring good news***!'*

Here we find a close connection between preaching and evangelistic activity. But this means that the role of the preacher is expanded - not that *gospelling* is narrowed down to only oral proclamation. Paul is talking about the prophets, who conveyed *good news* in dramatic and creative fashion, in many cases attempting even to embody the message they brought. The word about Christ is also the *event (rematos)* of Christ (v. 17), which needs to be *lived* and not just talked about.

Rom 15:18-20

For I will not dare to speak of anything except that which Christ has done through me to win a response from (all) the peoples - by word and deed, through the power of signs and wonders, through the power of the Spirit - so that from Jerusalem as far around as Illyricum the gospel of Christ has been established - making it my goal **to live the gospel** *not where Christ is named lest I build on another's foundation.*

Paul's evangelistic activity included word and deed, signs and wonders. Paul is talking about the range of his missionary labors and strategies, which come through clearly here:

- to work in an orderly way from Jerusalem around the Mediterranean coastline to the Adriatic;
- to organize communities of believers of any and all races *(ethne);*
- to work in new territories not yet entered by other missionaries or missionary teams.

All of these objectives are summarized in the phrase, *establish the gospel* (v. 19). (The fondness of translators for the term *preach* is evident, used here instead of the obvious *establish*, to translate *peplerokenai:* RSV, JB, NEB). In Romans 15, we have the remarkable picture of a man in his mid-fifties, after at least twenty years of struggle, hardship and itinerancy - twenty years of evangelistic activity - making plans for the next phase of his life (vv. 23-24).

CONCLUSIONS

Evangelistic activity for Paul involved concrete, specific actions in obedience to the crucified Messiah. Evangelism means action in service and not simply preaching. This seems especially clear in Galatians, which contains seven of the eighteen occasions when Paul uses the term, *euangelizomai*. The tenor of his statements in this letter reflects conflict and bitter disagreement over fundamentals. Paul is combating racism. [NOTE: Since 1981, my views have changed. I no longer believe that confronting *racism* was Paul's challenge in Galatia.]

Paul addresses himself in Galatians and elsewhere not (not only?) to preachers and other specialists in the churches. Paul is addressing ordinary people, who have been summoned through his witness to reverse their values and live a life of service and solidarity with Christ (Rom 8:16-18).

Paul did indeed preach Jesus but he did so in his lifestyle and in his work as a missionary-organizer and activist. If we can recover something of the intensity and challenge of Paul's faith we may in turn recover and rehabilitate that fine word, evangelism. The calling of the evangelist is not to revivalism or quietism but to *action*. Evangelism is an activity for all Christians and not just *preachers*.

All who are engaged in the Christian missionary enterprise, i.e., who are trying to live, with Paul, under the sign of the cross (II Cor 5), may find some practical help in Paul, as we see him more clearly as an organizer, who focused on concrete ways to get his job done. His first priority was to organize, to *plant* (I Cor 3) house churches. In the midst of these labors, which he shared with many co-workers (II Cor 1:19, Rom 16:7, etc.), Paul lived a vulnerable, risk-filled life. was in this context that he worked out his ideas and this context needs to be kept in mind as Paul's ideas are interpreted and applied to other situations in other times and places.

Paul is to be counted among those Christian thinkers-and-doers who call believers truly to live a life of service. Paul's successors today are Christian activists who meet the executed Messiah in the persons of the marginalized and oppressed, the sinned against, the struggling poor (I Cor 1:26-28). This is true apostolic succession, hearing and heeding Paul, the intense and passionate organizer of so long ago, who comes to us in letters which we know as Scripture and issues the challenge, *Imitate me!* (I Cor 4:16, 11:1, Phil 4:9). We are invited by Paul to become evangelists, that is, to adopt a lifestyle of vulnerability and risk and to build community with one another in the conviction that all of life and death are under the authority of the crucified Christ.

NOTES:

1. M. Dibelius and W. Kümmel. **Paul** (Philadelphia: Westminster Press, [19751), 68. A. Schweitzer. **The Mysticism of Paul the Apostle** (New York: Seabury Press [1968]), 156; J. Munck, **Paul and the Salvation of Mankind** (Atlanta: John Knox Press [1971]). 65. John Knox, **Chapters in a Life of Paul** (New York and Nashville: Abingdon Press [1955]). 103, E. Käsemann, **Perspectives on Paul** (Philadelphia: Fortress Press [1974]), 71.

2. **A Greek-English Lexicon of the New Testament**, Walter Bauer, W. Arndt, F.W. Gingrich, (Chicago, Cambridge: 1967, pages 317-318. 432.

PAUL TAKES A FIRST AT CAMBRIDGE

(A review of **The Cambridge Companion to St Paul**, James D.G. Dunn, Editor: Cambridge, United Kingdom (Cambridge University Press, 2003)

    This volume is one in a series of "Companions to Religion" which the publisher has been producing since 1997. Ten volumes have appeared with eight or more in progress. The book is composed of 18 essays, plus an excellent introduction by the editor. The topics include Paul's life and work, Paul's theology, a section entitled "St Paul" (which contains three essays devoted to Paul in the second century, Paul's legacy, and contemporary perspectives on Paul) and a section devoted to Paul's theology (which treats Paul's Jewish presuppositions, his gospel, christology, ecclesiology and ethics). Eight essays take up the Pauline letters, both of disputed and undisputed authorship, as well as the Pastorals. Not all of the contributions can be evaluated in this review.

    Considered together, these offerings accord with what could be called the British approach to Paul, that is, cautious scholarly conclusions founded on academic rigor. The essayists are not all British but all of their expositions are measured, well stated summations of a middling to moderately conservative treatment of Paul. Nothing wrong with that, but that is what you get in this book.

    James Dunn's introduction deftly summarizes much prior scholarship and suggests where research seems to be headed, primarily, Dunn thinks, into the areas of first century CE sociology and social dynamics. Dunn also anticipates (p. 11) new assessments, which will focus on Paul's ethics, Jewish mysticism, and the balance between divine initiative and human response in Paul's theology. The editor remarks (p. 12) upon what he describes as a "more radical" approach to Paul as exemplified first by Karl Barth's denigration of the so called History of Religions approach to Paul, and then by J. Louis Martyn's

1997 Galatians commentary. Dunn places Martyn upon the heights occupied by Karl Barth, because both want "to hear afresh the Gospel of Paul in all its raw power and offensiveness." This remark suggests to this reader that some important scholarly perspectives about Paul may have been left out of this volume. Barth and Martyn, theological high-wire acts, deserve more attention than they receive here. Barth's **Romans** did not even merit inclusion in the bibliography. Although Robert Morgan's brilliant essay on Paul's legacy (discussed below) partly corrects this volume's neglect of the results of earlier investigations, no scholar who might be described as "radical" is among the contributors to this volume.

Dunn singles out E. P. Sanders' emphasis upon Paul's debt to his Jewish heritage. Professor Dunn has himself contributed significantly to this "new perspective" by suggesting that Paul's primary dispute with Judaism was its refusal to extend covenant status to Gentiles. Not surprisingly, Dunn proposes (p. 10) his own conclusion as preferable to Sanders, who, Dunn claims, sees Paul as confused.

Ben Witherington assesses the state of Pauline studies today and takes note of four areas where much has been written: Jewish perspectives, feminist and liberationist perspectives, rhetorical studies and Paul's letters as scripture, to which Witherington adds his own critique. I wish Witherington had not felt it necessary to compliment (p. 260) Elizabeth Schüssler Fiorenza for her careful research. None of the male scholars he considers are treated in this patronizing manner. Instead, Witherington, or someone in this survey volume, ought to have addressed the faddishness of Pauline studies. Scholars in this field seem to fix upon a notion not because it builds upon previous discoveries but because the idea is simply a new but not necessarily a better way of recasting the fairly limited textual material. Narrowly erudite - even well packaged - restatements cannot expect a wide reading or a long shelf life, especially if they are not connected to earlier work.

A handful, at least, of arresting and idiosyncratic earlier perspectives on Paul are important and should not be neglected. Only two of the contributors to this volume, for example, make even a passing reference to Ernst Käsemann. The best answer to the neglect of Käsemann or any particular scholar is, of course, that this volume is a companion to the Apostle Paul and not to Käsemann. But in that case, an essay which neglects compelling and enduring observations by prior scholarship must stand on its hind legs and howl pretty convincingly all by itself.

The essays on Paul's life and missionary career (by Klaus Haacker and Stephen Barton, respectively) suffer from a tendency to give Acts greater weight than deserved as a source for the historical Paul. The relationship between Acts and the letters requires more nuance than perhaps is allowed in a summary treatment of Paul's life. Nevertheless, one would have expected the influence of Dibelius, John Knox, Bornkamm, Hans Conzelmann and Ernst Haenchen to have been more heavily felt. That Acts represents a Lukan and not a Pauline perspective seems to this reader to have been long ago established. Haacker does suggest certain episodes in Acts may have been "invented" and "some historical details" in Acts "remain doubtful" (p. 31) but he also believes (p. 19) Acts provides "historical knowledge." True. But about Paul? Burton assigns (p. 43) historicity to certain vignettes in Acts, such as the characterization of Paul as an exorcist. This observation demonstrates that once Acts rather than the letters is chosen as the first compass point to Paul, the further you travel the loster you will get.

Barton (p. 34) and Haacker (p. 19) take note of Paul having engaged in persecution of the Jesus messianists but they draw no inferences. L. W. Hurtado, in his lucid treatment of Paul's christology, does of course acknowledge (p. 188) that Paul confessed his attempts to "destroy" the messianists (Gal 1:13). Hurtado sees this as an occasion for much theological reflection by Paul, who was compelled, after his conversion, to reappraise his stance towards a "sect" he had previously considered "very dangerous" (p. 188). But absent from Hurtado, and from this volume is a consideration of the likelihood that Paul encountered crippling credibility problems among the messianists because of his past abuse of them. It is as if Paul's behavior in the very recent past left no impact at all among the messianic adherents he had tried to wipe out.

In his essay on Galatians, Bruce Longenecker concludes (p. 67) that, at Paul's conversion, "God took hold of Paul's life and made it an arena in which Christ himself became embodied." Writing of this flavor is not exegetical or even interpretative but rather sermonic. What, for example, are we to make of Paul's demand (Gal 4:21-31) that his antagonists in Galatia be cast out, as were the allegorical Hagar and her child? Is Paul's insistence upon the exclusion of persons the embodiment of Christ? Well, no. According to Longenecker, Paul is conducting a "playful reconfiguration of the scriptural story" (p. 72). Playful? Paul certainly is freely reordering the tradition but he is not playing games. I doubt if anyone can invoke a principle of interpretation in support of the proposition that when a Pauline comment is impossible to elucidate as a gem of theological enrichment then fun-loving Paul must be kidding! We should be open to the words on the page and draw the correct inference: some of Paul's comments are abusive of persons; others are inapplicable as ethical guide stars.

Brian Rosner's summary treatment of Paul's ethics does not get below the surface. It is superficially misleading to suggest that Paul merely counseled against "personal revenge" (p. 215) and favored "non-retaliation" as "the way of the cross" (p. 219). This overlooks the vitriolic Paul of Galatians who pronounced "Anathema!" upon his opponents and who hoped they would slash off their own penises. (Gal 1:8,9; 5:12).

Jerome Murphy O'Connor writes with magisterial command of the Corinthian material. His mastery lends heft to his thoughtful conclusions (p. 82) that Paul did not write I Cor 14:34-35 and that there is "no logic" in Paul's argument for the resurrection of the crucified Jesus. Unfortunately, this essay is marred by the still-too-common scholarly caricature of first century CE Judaism, whose adherents, Murphy O'Connor asserts (p. 76), suffered from "blind obedience to the commandments of Moses," which result in a "selfish inward-looking existence."

Robert Jewett's cogent treatment of Romans is thought provoking at a number of points. For example, Jewett asserts (p. 93) the letter is better understood as a "missionary document, not an abstract theological treatise." But this characterization of Romans is not entirely satisfactory as it does not fully account for all of the themes in the letter. In addition to looking for help in putting together a missionary campaign to Spain, Paul may have had other reasons to write to the Christians in Rome, including the desire to rehabilitate his reputation and to put into fixed form a thematic statement of his principles. Romans is a missionary document but it is sent to the already missionized.

Jewett detects (p. 92) what he calls Paul's reversal of "barriers of honor and shame in Greco-Roman culture." Jewett repeatedly alludes (pages 94, 95, 97, 98, 99, 100, 101) to the honor-shame convention and goes so far as to identify (103) evidence in Romans of an "early Christian revolution in the honor and shame system." The honor-shame hypothesis merits both a more detailed explication than it receives here and a citation to its source, if there is one other than Jewett. In fact, Jewett cites no secondary sources at all.

The challenge of summarizing Paul's opaque arguments may have been complicated by Jewett's efforts to combine his précis of Romans with his embrace of the honor-shame hypothesis. Take Romans 7. Is it the case, as

Jewett argues with reference to 7:19, that Paul became frustrated when his "zealous obedience" proved unable to produce "the good" (p. 97)? This conclusion sounds as an echo of Karl Barth's thunderous announcement in his commentary that Religion is Paul's great nemesis. But the focus on zealotry does not pay close enough attention to the assignation analogy in Romans 7:1-3.

The assignation analogy sets up Paul's argument, in the balance of the chapter. The humiliating, driving urgency of primal wanting is the antagonist Paul has in mind in Romans 7. Picture Paul or the designated letter-reader in Rome declaiming such easily-dramatized and emotionally fraught statements as "I am carnal!" "I don't know what I am doing!" "I do not do what I want!" "I hate what I do!" "Good is what I want to do -- but evil is what I actually do!" (vv. 14, 15, 19). These pleading, convulsive, defensive outcries ring in the ears not as the language of religion or of zealotry but as the language of passion.

Reminding the hearers of the hypothetical sexual adventurism Paul had just mentioned (vv. 1-3) and condemned (v.5), these emotional outbursts are an anguished acknowledgement that one's own conduct (from Paul's point of view) is both incomprehensible and hateful. Romans 7, therefore, cannot be explained as an expression of regret about the fruitlessness of a new-found zealotry. We know from other statements that Paul's all-consuming *new* devotion to an executed and resurrected Messiah commended to him a zealous demeanor, just as before - when he went after (Gal 1:13) the Messianists.

Alan Segal's sweeping explanations of Paul's Jewish "Presuppositions" are notably handicapped by limitations of space. A number of Segal's assertions require refinement or reinforcement, which is not given them here. Can we say, with Segal and without qualification, that Paul "continued to see himself as Jewish after his conversion to Christianity" (p. 161)? Then, precisely how is it that Paul's arguments are "distinctly Christian" though of a "particularly radical variety" (p. 163)? Is it the case that the pre-Christian Paul committed himself to "stamping out those who disagreed with him" because he "distrusted Gentiles and disliked any deviation as heresy" (p. 170)?

A half century ago, H.J. Schoeps took a very sharp trowel to this same ground in **Paul, The Theology of the Apostle in the Light of Jewish Religious History** (Philadelphia: Westminster, 1961). According to Schoeps, the messianic movement centered upon Jesus did not collapse "in despair, resignation or absurdity" because of Paul. (**Paul**, p. 120). This outcome was accomplished, Schoeps says, by way of Paul's exaltation of the Messiah "beyond all human proportions to the status of real divinity," which exaltation Schoeps sees as a "radical un-Jewish element" (**Paul**, p. 149) in Paul. According to Schoeps, in an assertion that may support Sanders against Dunn (see discussion above), Paul "was perhaps unable to perceive" Torah as indispensable to the Covenant (**Paul**, p. 213). Schoeps' ideas continue to be too important to be ignored.

Did Paul promote Jesus to a status of co-equal divinity with the God of the Hebrew scriptures? Or did Paul, after he joined the messianists and took a leading role in the mission to Gentiles, find the exaltation of Jesus already among their beliefs? In a thoughtful and fair-minded essay on Paul's christology, L. W. Hurtado credits (p. 196) Paul with elevating Jesus beyond messianic standing to divine status. Hurtado also believes (p. 191) the notion of Jesus "divine sonship" cannot be said to derive from "pagan ideas." Why not? Because the references to Jesus as God's son are "concentrated in Romans and Galatians" and therefore appear "where Paul is in most intense and sustained dialogue with the Jewish tradition." But the fact that Paul is in dialogue with "the Jewish tradition" in Galatians and Romans does not require the conclusion that Paul's designation of Jesus as God's son cannot come from "pagan ideas."

Luke Timothy Johnson's assignment in this volume is to treat Paul's ecclesiology. He does so with admirable clarity. But choices have to be made. In order to cover all of the "Pauline collection" (p. 211) Johnson takes up themes in the disputed letters and the pastorals, which he sees as "genuine lines of continuity" (p. 199) in all of the letters. This approach leads to very general conclusions (p. 211), as Johnson is obliged to place a reduced emphasis upon certain motifs found only in the undisputed letters, such as Paul's choleric insistence upon his personal authority and his neglect of any reference to a hierarchy beyond the local assembly.

Johnson maintains that "God is capable of acting outside God's own scriptural precedents" (p. 202). Paul certainly felt this way and was compelled more than once to defend himself in response to the question it raises: who has the authority to decide when God has acted? The ordered ecclesiastical response to this question, beginning shortly after Paul's death if not before, is that a structure external to the local community was required. This is the only conceivable development if due account was to be taken of the need for doctrinal and scriptural consensus, resistance to regional and not simply local persecution, institutional survival beyond one or two generations and the prevalence of new "prophets," who claimed to mediate the Spirit to the little congregations they visited.

As C. J. Roestzel suggests in his cogent essay on Paulinists in the Second Century CE, Paul as Establishmentarian was invoked over against interpreters such as Marcion who wanted to use Paul's statements to disconnect faith in Jesus Christ from history. Ironically enough, the various gyrations upon his legacy by ecclesiastically-minded thinkers permitted the perplexing letters of the apocalyptically-minded Paul to survive and enter the canon.

What does this rich volume offer in the way of an assessment of Paul's legacy? Each of the essays may be said to make a contribution here, but special attention is owed to Robert Morgan's splendid essay. Morgan's exposition is both perceptive and wise. He points out that the source of the continuing power of Paul's legacy is not the influence of his letters upon Christian doctrine but the fact that the letters "partly constitute this religion" (p. 242).

The exegesis of Paul's letters attends to his legacy not primarily through technical details but through interaction "with the practice of the religion" (p. 242). Morgan lays creative emphasis upon "the canonical factor" (p. 244) of the letters and argues, convincingly, that historical study and interpretation of Paul is "transient" because what endures are "the epistles themselves" (p. 246). This may explain why Pauline scholarship may appear faddish. It is inherently provisional and contingent (see discussion above). Each generation requires restatements of different aspects of Paul's legacy. Morgan suggests the impact of Paul's letters is likely always to be mediated through faith. Paul would probably be indifferent to the fact that the letters are "public property" in our post-theistic world "unless he thought that by becoming a post-theist to the post-theists he might by all means save some" (p. 254).

Cuándo merecieron mis descuidos
Ocupar vuestros cuidados?

When has my carelessness
Proved worthy of your care?

-

Juana Ramírez
Sor Juana Inés de la Cruz

"I CANNOT LISTEN TO THIS ANYMORE"

Berlin Diaries, 1940-1945 by Marie Vassilchikov (New York: Knopf, 1987)

"29 January, 1940 . . . My office does not seem to know who its Top Boss is, as everybody is giving orders at the same time, although the Reich's Propaganda Minister, Dr. Joseph Goebbels, is said to have the last word" (page 5).

Diaries can be a valuable antidote to the treacheries of memory and the self-interest of hindsight. But the trouble is, many such journals are boring. Plus, many important events unfold without the benefit of the keen-eyed and conscientious diarist. One such compulsive diarist was Marie Vassilchikov (1917-1978), daughter of a minor Russian nobleman, whose family was evicted from Russia in 1919 and who found herself trapped in Hitler's Europe at the outbreak of the Second World War. Her journal has recently been published as *Berlin Diaries, 1940-1945*. This document, edited after her death by her brother George, is of great importance.

Brilliant, multilingual, independent, and with an eye for the telling detail, "Missie" worked for several German propaganda and information offices throughout the war. She typed many of her observations in English during office hours and concealed the pages first in file cabinets and later in various spots in and around Berlin.

Missie's diary provides an eyewitness account of the Allied bombing of Berlin, which was undertaken in retaliation for an accidental German bombing of London on August 24, 1940. From the diary: "10 October, 1940 . . . This evening I was at a party when the alarm sounded. The shooting was very loud and poor Maxchen Kieckebusch, whose nerves have gone to pieces since he was injured in the spine in France, rolled on the floor moaning, *Ich kann das nicht mehr Horen* [I cannot listen to this anymore] over and over again" (p. 32).

We read of the disintegration of the matrix of ordinary life: an elderly postman dies and is laid out for a week on the kitchen table before being taken away. At one end of the table near the feet of the corpse, sandwiches are prepared and given to a rescue party looking for persons alive under the rubble of the latest Allied bombing. Before the end of the war all the gravediggers had been called into the army. Relatives had to bury their dead in cardboard coffins.

How important is this book? From it we learn much about aristocratic Germans who detested Hitler and who conspired to kill him. Successive plots were discussed and planned, and at least one was bravely and naively attempted; a suitcase fined with explosives was planted in Hitler's underground headquarters. With the failure of this attempt, the most active conspirators were rounded up, together with their families, associates, and acquaintances.

Unbelievably, the conspirators had made long lists of those who would be invited to join the post-Hitler German government. The discovery of these lists led to the arrest and execution of more than eleven thousand persons in 1944 and the first five months of 1945. The theologian and pastor Dietrich Bonhoeffer was among these last. Several conspirators escaped Nazi detection only to be captured by the advancing Red Army. They disappeared forever in the Russian Gulag.

Missie was informed of the conspiracy to execute Hitler and may have given more to the various plots than just her sympathy. Her diary of these events is the only firsthand account known to exist. It astonishes that a Russian woman living in Berlin and identified with anti-Hitler conspirators, somehow avoided suspicion, arrest, and execution. Her diary is a rare and remarkable document.

THAT WHICH YOU HAVE BEEN GIVEN YOU MUST ALSO USE

Roger's Version by John Updike
New York: Knopf, 1986

Have you ever attended the wedding of an unbelieving couple who, for family reasons alone, desire the matrimonial ministrations of the clergy? If so, you can identify with John Updike's description of a minister who "has a way of intoning empty phrases so that not a pinfeather of the agnostic couple's integrity is ruffled while the bride's staunchly Episcopalian step-grandmother (who doesn't hear too well anyway) leaves the service also placated."

John Updike hits close to home with *Roger's Version*. Updike's straightforward style is well suited to descriptive prose, but there is more to this book than a look at pale and pleasant Christian theology and practice. The issue before Updike is an old one. If everything in creation has its sublime purposes, what is the connection between sexuality and faith? Tertullian, father of the Trinitarian framework of Christian theology, provides the basis for Roger's version of theology/sexuality: that which you have been given, you must also use.

The earthy confessions of the middle-aged patristics professor Roger Lambert move along unexpected paths and provoke the reader's response. A few examples among many-. "The genius of Calvinism has been to make property an outward sign and a sacred symbol." If that statement doesn't get you into the dialogue, Roger's description of a Quaker colleague might do it: "He believed nothing you could put into writing." Roger on his favorite reading matter: "I have a secret shame. I always feel better - cleaner, revitalized - after reading theology. Lest you take me for a goody-goody, I find kindred comfort and inspiration in pornography."

Updike has not overlooked the *solo fides* aficionado: "The Devil is the absence of doubt. He's what pushes people into suicide bombing, into setting up extermination camps. Doubt may give your dinner a funny taste, but it's faith that goes out and kills."

There is political commentary as well. Ronald Reagan was the choice of many of the faithful because "he asked so little and promised so much . . . perfecting his imitation of the Heavenly Presider, whose inactivity has held our loyalty for two millennia." On the scandal of resurrection faith: "What is in worst taste, being circumcised or being crucified? Being laid in a manger or in a tomb?"

For some this novel is ill mannered and pornographic. Updike seems prepared for that response. The plot is overloaded with Roger Lambert's sexual fantasies as Roger fools around with Tertullian's dictum: "the body is for the eternal enjoyment of the soul." Thus human activity, including sex and despite the "depressing mechanics" of it all, is a sign of "our eternal survival."

SHALL THE DEAD RULE THE LIVING?

Ironweed by William Kennedy
New York: Penguin Books, 1987

Why review a book, which was published years ago? **Ironweed** is now in paperback and has been adapted to film. These factors combine to bring the Pulitzer Prize winner within both the budget and the wider circle of interest of many readers.

The novel is the third part of William Kennedy's Albany cycle. (The earlier books are **Legs** and **Billy Phalen's Greatest Game**.) **Ironweed** traces the return of a man *to* his hometown in 1937 after a twenty-year absence. Francis Phalen deserted his family after the accidental death of his infant son. He has spent two decades on the bum.

William Kennedy's gifts as a writer are apparent in the crafting of dialogue. (Kennedy also wrote the screenplay for the film, which offers crisp and arresting lines for Jack Nicholson and Meryl Streep.) The compressed conversation of Kennedy's ruined characters allow an unexpected impact from a phrase of no more than two or three words. Francis and his pal Rudy are together after Francis's visit to his son's grave (p. 20):

> "Whatayou been up to?" Rudy asked. "You know somebody buried up there?"

"A little kid I used to know."

"A kid? What'd he do, die young?"

"Pretty young."

"What happened to him?"

"He fell."

"He fell where?"

"He fell on the floor."

"Hell I fall on the floor about twice a day

and I ain't dead."

"That's what you think," Francis said.

Kennedy is attempting to trace the emotional struggles that unfold on the battleground of Francis Phalen's interior world. Francis encounters ghosts from his past - his dead son, men he has killed, his parents buried in the family plot - as well as his wife. These encounters focus on Francis's attempt to understand the impulses that caused him to flee Albany and now to return.

Kennedy allows the dead son, Gerald, to articulate (p. 19) to the reader what is at stake for Francis. Gerald, through an act of silent will, imposed on his father the pressing obligation to perform his final acts of expiation for abandoning the family.

"You will not know, the child silently said, what these acts are until you have performed them all. And after you have performed them you will not understand that they are expiatory any more than you have understood all the other expiation that has kept you in such prolonged humiliation. Then, when these final acts are complete, you will stop trying to die because of me."

Kennedy is concerned that the reader gets the point early and read on for other reasons. What might these be? The awareness of guilt; the manner in which unknowing expiation occurs; the security that comes from well-deserved punishment, which is self-inflicted and certain.

Does expiation compel humiliation? Can expiation occur without understanding? Do the dead - whether family or martyred saints of God - rule the living? Are the dead entitled to exercise this power?

PASS BOLDLY INTO THAT OTHER WORLD

"The Dead" by James Joyce
In **Dubliners**. New York: Viking Press, 1967

Some reissues are worth a second or third critical review. This is the case with anything by James Joyce, whose story "The Dead" has recently been brought out again by several publishers in connection with the release of John Huston's film adaptation.

"The Dead" is a precise and sensitive description of a dinner party hosted by two elderly sisters in their Dublin home on January 6, 1904, the Feast of the Epiphany. Gabriel Conroy and his wife Greta attend the dance hosted by his aunts. This is an annual event for them. In fact, the successful and articulate Gabriel is expected as usual to offer the toast at dinner and so to set the right tone for the occasion. Gabriel does so but feels anxious to discharge this responsibility properly with just the right amount of humor and good taste. Gabriel must also carve the turkey and perform other manly duties, such as the protection of decorum from the drunken presence of an alcoholic relative. Gabriel does well, knows that he does well. Gabriel knows, in fact, that always he has done well and has become a decent, respected Irishman. But he cannot be himself - express his own needs and emotions.

As he observes his sleeping wife and reflects on the evening just spent with his elderly aunts, Gabriel knows that death cannot be far from him or from any of them. What then? What now? What steps might he take to use more fully the unknowable portion of time remaining to him? "Better," Gabriel concludes, "pass boldly into that other world, in the full glory of some passion, than fade and wither dismall with age" (p. 223). Gabriel, unable to overcome a lifetime of restraint, can do no more - he chooses to do no more - than slip quietly into bed. For James Joyce, one joins the company of "the dead" when the emotional life is suppressed.

Cesar Chavez
1927-1993

Grandpa Cesario had been a slave in Mexico
until he escaped in 1880 and came to Texas

At the Forty Acres one afternoon,
I introduce Cesar to my father
They face each other
Mirrors
Eye contact at eye level
Phallic-lensed cameras
around their necks . . .

"As far as I am concerned these people do not
exist," says Arizona Governor Jack Williams.
Who made a law to give a union a
*   rough time organizing.*
Cesar retaliates with a "fast of love"   . . .
The Gov sat out his term
The law wasn't changed.
But the people were.
The people were.

Excerpts from *Where We Came From,*
Portrait – 1969, and *Fasting Again: Arizona*
Fields of Courage
By
Susan Samuels Drake

(BUT TO . . .) KNOW THE MIND OF GOD

A Brief History of Time by Stephen Hawking, Bantam Books, 1988

Stephen W. Hawking is a theoretical physicist who holds the post at Cambridge University once held by Isaac Newton. Hawking writes of attending a conference on cosmology at the Vatican in 1981. At the end of the conference the pope cautioned that scientists should not examine the moment of the creation of the universe because that was the work of God. In his book Stephen Hawking has not heeded the pope's advice. One of his conclusions is that we now have a picture of developments "to about one second after the Big Bang" (p. 118). For Hawking, scientific inquiry has moved from "what" questions right on through to "how" and is at the point of answering "why." As soon as theorists succeed in incorporating the law of gravity into a properly developed and tested grand unification theory (GUT) we will then "know the mind of God" (p. 175).

Hawking writes carefully for the non-specialist. He has taken the trouble to provide a glossary with page references. He has avoided mathematical formulas and has worked hard to find analogies for the abstractions of twentieth-century physics. The universe looks the same from all directions, "rather like a balloon with a number of spots painted on it, being steadily blown up. As the balloon expands, the distance between any two spots increases, but there is no spot that can be said to be the center of the expansion" (p. 42).

Any careful reader can use Hawking's little book (198 pages including introduction, glossary, index, and three excursi on Einstein, Galileo, and Newton) to participate in ongoing discussions about a number of questions that are asked these days primarily by children and physicists. What is nature, and where did it come from? What is time? Is it possible to move backward in time? Is there a beginning or a boundary to the universe? Will the universe come to an end, and what kind of end will it be? What did God do in the beginning, and what role does God play now in the physical world?

The answers to such questions, Hawking believes, are to be found in the inquiries of theoretical physicists. For Hawking, the core of modern physics is quantum mechanics, the development of theories having to do with the movement and the components of energy, as distinguished from classical physics, the study of the properties of matter. Hawking states that quantum physics underlies nearly all of modern science and development, including nuclear power and micro technology and asserts that quantum physics will eventually not only explain the origin of every thing but also predict the future.

A number of ideas compressed into this small book warrant further examination. Hawking writes of a "survival advantage" (p. 12) scientific discovery has conveyed to humankind that can be canceled by further discoveries that "may destroy us all" (p. 12). Life in our sector of the galaxies developed because of disorder in matter that disrupted the generally smooth character of the universe. Hawking suggests that intelligent beings can exist only in an expanding universe. The idea here is that scientific laws are predictable in only one direction through time and that a collapsing universe would cause a reversal of the "arrows of time" (pp. 143 f.) and would thus invalidate human comprehensibility. Hawking speculates about a notion called "the anthropic principle" (p. 124), which appears to mean that the universe is as it is because, if it were not, we would not be around to observe it. But if the anthropic principle is the bottom line then scientific cosmology has become anthropology, and why waste any more time with telescopes or particle accelerators? Hawking suggests that the universe (time and space taken together) is "finite yet without boundary" (p. 136). This is the most arresting and, as yet unprovable of Stephen Hawking's proposals, but he is willing to wait for further observations that may move this idea to a higher degree of probability.

In the midst of all this theorizing Hawking conveys something of the playfulness of many who are engaged in the quantum physics quest. There is mention of a now-discarded theory known as LGM 1-4, LGM standing for "little green men." The explosion that is supposed to have kicked off our expanding universe is commonly known as the Big Bang. The smallest known particles are called quarks and come in flavors; the uniform nature of collapsing stars goes by the maxim "black holes have no hair." (p. 92)

Because theoretical physics has turned very precisely toward the whys of life, theology and ethics will have to pay closer attention. I will give two examples. When did time begin? Hawking offers the idea of a "singularity," a unique event in time at which the laws of science break down and predictability disappears. The Big Bang, therefore, is a singularity, and it may be said that time began with creation itself. From this it follows that time will come to an end when the universe ceases its expansion, collapses into itself, and perhaps sets off another Big Bang. The singularity idea has many implications for the theological dimensions of eschatology as well as for cosmology.

An example of the importance of quantum physics for ethics might be the "uncertainty principle" of Werner Heisenberg (1926), which Hawking refers to as "a fundamental, inescapable property of the world" (p. 55). Briefly, the uncertainty principle asserts that the position and velocity of particles cannot be precisely predicted. Rather, particles exist in a quantum state, which is a combination of position and velocity and which suggests a range of possible locations where particles are likely to be found. This means that we do not live in a deterministic universe where definite results can be expected. This also suggests there is a limit to our capacity to know what is going on.

If results in science are subject to randomness, ought not this principle of uncertainty be recognized when we speak of "good" and "bad" behavior? Isn't it less pretentious and more helpful to think in terms of *quantum ethics,* which would allow for a range of appropriate actions? I think this kind of approach is in harmony with Jesus' comments about ethical behavior. When asked about the greatest of God's commands he cited the *Shemah* (Deut. 6:4) and added that "you shall love your neighbor as yourself" (Mark 12:29-30). This admonition finds parallels in many traditions and leaves much room for intelligent, responsible reflection-action.

Theoretical physics awaits and accepts the judgment of the future, whose discoveries and experiments either prove, or dismiss earlier claims. The author cites many instances of this: even the supernovas of physics, Newton and Einstein, admitted earlier mistakes or had their ideas corrected by others. Most theological reflection, on the other hand, lacks any sort of empirical reference. In other words, theological speculations, disconnected as they are from a close reading of "secular" history, normally make predictions that do not have to agree with observation.

In the last ten years or so theoretical physics has turned cosmology into a subject for scientific discussion and discovery. Can theological speculation accept the challenge of quantum physics and adapt to the conceptual limits that are laid down? Are seminaries prepared to train pastors and teachers to pay attention to the quanta discussions? How might theocentric statements be tested and then sustained or discarded? These are a few of the questions that quantum physics has placed on the theological agenda.

A SPIRITUAL BAKED POTATO

The Countertife, by Philip Roth
New York: Penguin Books, 1988

Nathan Zuckerman, Jewish writer, husband of several gentile wives, a guy who believes that thinking about things matters, this literary invention of Philip Roth, works out his own death and life on paper. Zuckerman pieces together his fate and then takes it apart in varied settings: New York, Israel, and England; at the Wailing Wall, airborne, at a carol service in London's West End - "it was as though they were symbolically feasting upon, communally devouring, a massive spiritual baked potato" (p. 295).

For Philip Roth identity issue takes shape in very personal terms. Zuckerman the Jew is ambivalent about ritual circumcision. He insists it be performed on his son, yet he sees circumcision as proof that "the heavy hand of human values falls upon you right at the start..." (P. 370). He is revolted by both the intensities of Israeli Semitism and the subtleties of London's anti-Semitism: "the land of the shootout" and "the land of the carol service" (P. 336). He lives not in Israel but in the Diaspora because he likes it.

An awareness of Jewish history, Jewish pain, is ever present, the pain of those who "couldn't go on being themselves without inciting to violence ominous forces against which they hadn't the slightest means of defense" (p. 59).

Disharmony and discord is everywhere in this book. Yet there is acceptance. The Israeli zealot on the kibbutz, the cynical Jerusalem journalist, the detached wordsmith from New Jersey concede nothing yet arrive at a tense accommodation to each other's Jewishness.

Everyone has sharp human edges here. A mistress or wife is more than an occasion for fantasizing or a foil for rebellion against domesticity. These women challenge the premises and the behavior of the Zuckerman brothers, the semi-famous novelist Nathan, over committed to the idea of meaning-through-observation, and the thoroughly professional and depressed dentist Henry, over committed to the idea of fulfillment-through-liberation/resignation.

Roth drives home his points with lucidity and assertiveness. Of course there are contradictions: "What matters isn't what made you do it but what you do" (p. 158). "Anybody can run away and survive; the trick was to stay and survive" (p. 268). "Life is the adventure of losing your way" (p. 147). Philip Roth's work exemplifies the integrity of serious imaginative writing that puzzles out life's incapacities and joys.

QUAINT BUT CREDIBLE

Toyohiko Kagawa: Apostle of Love and Social Justice by Robert Schildgen
Berkeley: Centenary Books, 1988

Can a human life be captured between the covers of a book? The biographer's challenge has been met in this well-researched and carefully written book by Robert Schildgen. With access to Kagawa associates and family members, as well as government and private archives, Schildgen has crafted an important document.

The story of this life parallels the transformation of modem Japan. Grandson of a samurai, son of a geisha concubine, Toyohiko Kagawa (1888-1960) lived through one of the most turbulent epochs in Japanese history. Kagawa was an active participant in the three major phases of this development, the wrenching transition from economic isolation (1868-1931), the period of militaristic and nationalistic expansion (1932-1945), and the carefully planned postwar creation of the Japanese industrial state. A gifted son of modern Japan and a devotee of an alien religion, Kagawa spent his life struggling to discover what faith in Jesus could mean for Japan.

While an adolescent, Kagawa became a Christian and thereafter tried to live as he imagined any follower of Jesus ought to live. Never one for halfway measures, the young Kagawa gave his energies to the slum dwellers of Kobe. He poured himself into a solitary effort to live with beggars, prostitutes, alcoholics, and mentally ill people who inhabited the wastelands of the newly industrialized city.

Kagawa's devotion to a Franciscan ideal of self-sacrifice was matched by his paradoxical efforts to build an empire of public-spirited agencies and organizations. Advocating women's suffrage, collective bargaining, economic development, socialism, and pacifism, Kagawa helped establish labor unions, newspapers, political parties, and cooperatives. He wrote best-selling novels, theological treatises, and poetry. He preached tirelessly throughout Japan, and, as his fame spread, Kagawa preached throughout the world.

Japan was also changing. During the 1920s the power of militaristic elements in Japanese society was beginning to overwhelm all opposition, including Kagawa. Ultranationalists eventually took complete control and led the nation into a bloody occupation of Manchuria in 1931, war with China in 1937, and war with the United States in 1941. As early as 1922, Kagawa was forbidden to speak abroad except on preaching missions. He endured years of official harassment and eventually he was silenced and then imprisoned.

Kagawa was fundamentally a patriot. During the 1930s, Kagawa consistently denounced Japanese expansionism, but he told an associate that if war came he would support it (p. 228). When war did come he was shocked by and publicly denounced the U.S. bombing of Japanese cities, which killed hundreds of thousands of his fellow citizens. He made other nationalistic propaganda statements, but said later that he felt forced into the role of propagandist by U.S. actions.

After the war, Kagawa was appointed national food commissioner and became an adviser to the first postwar cabinet. He also renewed his national and international speaking tours, established a number of new social welfare organizations, and wrote and translated several books. He spent the final years of his life an advocate for world peace.

In the hero-worshiping West, Toyohiko Kagawa was at one time as well known as Albert Schweitzer. Yet today Kagawa is little remembered. Perhaps this failure of collective memory is due to Kagawa's wartime conduct. Or perhaps direct action supported by an ethic of service to others seems more quaint than credible in times of tight budgets and self-absorption.

Kagawa's life highlights the tension between the certainty of the converted and the ambiguities of life in a particular place and time. Kagawa wished to be loyal to Japan but was contemptuous of patriotic hysteria. He admired the West but he scorned its racism and colonialism. He believed in nonviolence, yet he participated in the affairs of a world rushing heedlessly into war. A Christian in a culture older than Christianity, a pacifist in a militaristic society, an activist where activism was not acceptable, a slum worker and also a visionary empire builder, Kagawa's own words may best sum up his life: "I am a free-lance, a tramp, a vagabond for Christ . . . . I go like the wind" (p. 261).

We would do well to take more note of him.

Así, cuando yo mía
Te llamo, no pretendo
Que juzguen que eres mía
Sino sólo que yo ser tuya quiero

I do not pretend
Some may judge thee mine
When I so name Thou,
Yet may I be Thine

Juana Ramírez
Sor Juana Inés de la Cruz

DISCERNMENT... NOT DOCTRINE

The Rain in the Trees, by W. S. Merwin
New York: Knopf, 1988

The poet W. S. Merwin lives in Hawaii. In these poems, he applies his craft to the ancient island culture whose own language has all but disappeared. The poet is aware of cultural destruction inherent in the continuing Western occupation of the islands. Merwin suggests that even the use of the English language is an act of violence in this setting. The importation of alien symbols seems an unwarranted intrusion. But what else can an English-speaking Western poet do? One must use the tools of the conqueror, which are also one's own and one's only tools. The other tools are broken.

> *when they start to use your language*
> *do they say what you say*
> *who are they in your words . . .*
>
> *When they are converted to your gods*
> *do they know who they are praying to*
> *do you know who is praying*
> ("Conqueror" p. 62)
>
> *Many of the things the words were about*
> *no longer exist*
> *the noun for standing in mist by a*
> *haunted tree*
> *the verb for I.*
> ("Losing a Language" p. 67)

Merwin insists upon the connection between power and language. Because peoples disappear from history, "dictionaries are full of graves" (p. 30).

Survivors, Merwin suggests, having lost their language, have also lost the will to live.

> *The children will not repeat*
> *the phrases their parents speak*
> *somebody has persuaded them*
> *that it is better to say everything*
> *differently*
> *so that they can be admired somewhere*
> *farther and farther away*
> ("Losing a Language" p. 67)

The connection between power and words is like the connection between life and memory. One does not live well but can only hope to "manage" (p. 15) when the connection is severed. And the losses affect both the conquered and the conquerors.

> *If only you had written our language*
> *we would have remembered how you*
> *died . . .*
>
> *you would have survived*
> *as we do*
>
> *we might have believed*
> *in a homeland*
> ("The Lost Originals" p. 68)

Merwin wants to write in the new language he is discovering ("Witness," p. 65), but he appears to know that he cannot. The old language is alien, and all the words have been used "for other things" (p. 5).

Nevertheless, the poet continues to believe in the possibility of personal integrity. There is a sturdy stubbornness in this man, who has been writing good, resilient verses for many decades and who believes in new beginnings in new places.

> *we thought we were younger*
> *through all those ages of knowing*
> *nothing*
> *and there you are . . .*
> *now we have only the age that is left*
> *to be together. . .*
> *for the rest of our lives*
> ("Before Us" p. 30)

Merwin asks if there can be personal harmony in the midst of cultural dissonance. Merwin is not a romantic poet, whose lesser calling smoothes out the roughness of every day. Nor is he narrowly ideological, which would limit the appreciation of his work to soon forgotten times and places. Merwin is focused on perception, not doctrine. When the experience rings true, the perception rings true. The application of words to experience demands attention and offers comfort.

> *You are going for a long time*
> *and nobody knows what to expect*
>
> *we are trying to learn*
> *not to accompany gifts with advice*
>
> *or to suppose we can protect you*
> *from being changed . . .*

("For the departure of a stepson" p. 54)

SO LONG

To conclude, I announce what comes after me.

I remember I said before my leaves sprang at all,

I would raise my voice jocund and strong with reference to consummations.

When America does what was promis'd,

. . .

Then to me and mine our due fruition

Walt Whitman

Songs of Parting
Leaves of Grass

A SHRILL ARGUMENT, THEN BLOOD

Battle Cry of Freedom: The Civil War Era, by James M. McPherson. New York: Oxford University Press, 1988

James McPherson has written a fine history of the Civil War. This dramatic period of American history can be treated as a numbing series of military and political events, but McPherson's narrative approach permits the reader to work smoothly through the material. The volume aims to be comprehensive and contains photos and maps of military campaigns and battles.

McPherson opens the curtain on the nation in 1850. In this way he is able to identify the cause of the war: a shrill sectional argument about the extension of slavery across the American continent. The final phase of this generations-old debate began when President Polk started a war with Mexico in order to secure Texas. Henry Clay and other Whigs, including a one-term ex-congressman from Illinois, Abraham Lincoln, objected to the acquisition of additional territory unless slavery was prohibited. Polk's critics insisted that human slavery was incompatible with the westward expansion of the nation. Southern leaders insisted that the slave-holding South must survive even at the cost of separation from the other states. The extreme Southern position enabled the enemies of slavery to win over the electorate by arguing that slavery posed a deadly threat to free labor and secession an equally dangerous threat to the future of the nation. The cogency of this attack propelled Lincoln into the White House in 1860.

Why did the North win the war? McPherson gives his reasons, including superior northern leadership, a strategy of total war employed by Grant and Sherman, and the industrial and numerical advantages enjoyed by the North. One of the greatest values of the book is its interpretative key: contingency. McPherson indicates how the course of events might have been changed at different points and leaves the reader to speculate. Suppose Robert

E. Lee had developed a larger military vision than the Virginia countryside? Suppose England had not been so wary of French influence in America and had recognized the Confederacy right away? Suppose Lincoln had not issued the Emancipation Proclamation in 1862, a gesture that transformed the struggle into a fight for human freedom? Suppose Lincoln had been motivated more by expediency than by principle and had not pressed the issue to ultimate military victory?

What were the consequences of the war? Among the most important were that the principal of secession was killed along with slavery. After 1865, the central government began to dominate the life of the nation. McPherson points out that eleven of the first twelve Constitutional amendments limited the central government before the Civil War and that six of the next seven amendments expanded federal governmental authority. Federal court jurisdiction was expanded, a national currency and banking and tax systems were created. A truly national economy began to develop.

McPherson also points to a shift in political power from South to North, which made the United States less like the rest of the world. War-stimulated industrial development laid the foundation for United States world leadership for the next one hundred years. McPherson suggests that many of these changes were symbolized as "the United States" became a singular noun. "Nation" replaced "union" in Lincoln's vocabulary and in common parlance.

This book is part of a new Oxford Press series of the history of the United States edited by C. Vann Woodward. What a pleasure to read an important and thoughtful book that combines valuable insights with clear, fluid writing. (In 1989, this book received the Pulitzer Prize in History.)

A DICHOTOMY THAT WON'T DI

Paul Beyond the Judaism / Hellenism Divide,
Engberg-Pedersen, Troels, editor
Louisville: Westminster John Knox, 2001

When applied to Paul and his environment, the terms Judaism and Hellenism are "strongly ideological" (page 3). So states the editor of this volume. And if true, editor Troels Engberg-Pedersen asserts, NT Scholarship should "give up altogether operating with the dichotomy." The Apostle Paul himself apparently thought the terms should be tossed. Paul wrote (Gal 3:28) "there is neither Jew nor Greek." But wait a minute. Paul is using the very categories he claims are no longer valid. What does Paul mean?

You will not find out in this book. Unfortunately, the essayists have been limited (page 15) to Paul's Corinthian correspondence. This restriction is bound to render incomplete the promise of the title of this volume. Even though the contributors have not given the evidence of Galatians and Romans the same weight as First and Second Corinthians, each one has to contend with the possibility that conceptual categories, even when dismissed as inapplicable, remain analytically helpful. The contributors recognize this because they have not followed the editor's recommendation that the Hellenism-Judaism dichotomy be discarded.

The essays are uniformly of high quality and nuanced in their approach to the "Judaism/Hellenism Divide." Wayne Meeks has supplied two essays. In one of them he lays emphasis upon the variety of cultural forms in early Christian groups and states (page 26): "The adjectives Jewish and Hellenistic are practically no help at all in sorting out that variety." Note that Meeks would limit his cashiering of the concepts to their use as adjectives. The idea is to get down to a noun. The other contributors found their own ways to traverse the "Divide."

Henrik Tronier, argues (page 167) convincingly, that Paul is adapting to an apocalyptic framework, concepts found in his Hellenistic milieu. The framework itself, Tronier correctly suggests, is just as much a product of that milieu as the concepts Paul adapts. But at the same time, Tronier says, Paul is to be "firmly situated" in his "immediate Jewish context," which is defined here as "Jewish apocalypticism" which is "itself a particular version and variation of certain basic ideas in the Hellenistic world at large, Jewish as well as non-Jewish" (page 167). Overlooking the circular confusion of this observation, Tronier goes on to assert (page 195) that Paul is concerned not about anthropological descriptions but about the source of knowledge. This insight, which is a significant contribution to the understanding of the fragmentary Corinthian correspondence, does not depend upon Tronier's previous argument that everything is "Hellenistic."

Between his everything-is-Hellenistic argument and his conclusion that Paul's main focus is to draw attention to his interlocutors' failure to think straight, Tronier suggests (page 168) that certain perceived dichotomies (religion-versus-philosophy, space-vs.-time, Hellenistic-vs.-Jewish/Christian world views) should be replaced (page 182) by a "cognitive dualism" between the wisdom of this world and the wisdom of God. This proposal is not convincing. The replacement of the older sets of supposed opposites by a single remaining dualism may not be an advance in our understanding of Paul. Paul himself thought and argued in dichotomous terms. He told the Corinthians, for example, that Jews need "signs" while Greeks "seek wisdom" (I Cor 1:22). The Hellenistic / Jewish "divide" seems still to be an appropriate way to think about Paul's own perspective and the contingent issues he confronted.

Margaret H. Mitchell focuses her contribution on Paul's efforts to win converts by way of a program of accommodation to the expectations of his missionary targets. Mitchell's attention is drawn to Paul's claim to be (as the occasion warranted) "all things to all people" (I Cor 9:19-23). Mitchell concentrates her discussion upon earlier interpreters of Paul (Tertullian, Clement of Alexander, Origin, and Chrysostom) as well as Paul's older contemporary, Philo. Mitchell argues that Paul probably was influenced by "Hellenistic traditions" though these must have been "integrated with other elements of his thought" (page 201) including "Hellenistic Jewish assumptions and reappropriations" (page 214).

Is comprehension gained by calling everything "Hellenistic?" Isn't it the case that early Christian groups "may be defined historically or sociologically in this way or that?" See Eduard Schweizer, (**Church Order in the New Testament** (SCM, 1961, page 95). Shouldn't the classification of these groups be seen as a preliminary and tentative exercise, which leads to a discussion of what was hoped to be created: a localized center for the celebration and worship of Messiah Jesus?

David E. Aune seems to assert (page 215), *contra* Tronier, that Paul's "eschatological or apocalyptic thought" is rooted in Judaism. Aune at first uses these terms interchangeably but then confuses this reader by speaking of "early Jewish apocalypses" as distinct from "Hellenistic eschatology" (page 217). Aune then once again merges the terms and states that "apocalyptic eschatology" also included "early Christian forms" (218). There is too much shuffling of adjectives here. Is this the result of editorial insistence that every contributor announce the demise of the "Divide?" The practical demarcation Aune sees is a more pronounced communal destiny in the apocalyptic (Jewish) form and a greater concentration on individual fate in the eschatological (Hellenistic) form. F.C. Baur, much criticized by two of the contributors to this volume (pages 18-19, 32-37), probably would have agreed.

Once freed from the need to array cosmological terminology along the Jewish / Hellenistic Divide, Aune delivers (pages 220-234) an original and helpful exegesis of 2 Cor 4:16-5:10. Aune is especially good at 4:16, where a Platonic antithesis (the outer container / the soul) is clothed in a metaphor of duality coined by Paul to distinguish the mortal, physical body from a person's enduring spirit: the outer person / the inner person. Aune believes the Platonic antithesis may have been mediated to Paul via Philo or (more likely) some popular platonic philosophy. In this, he shows he is in agreement with Tronier's contention, after all, that most everything in Paul can be said to be *Hellenistic*. Aune finds other evidence of Hellenistic usage and influence: "tent" (page 224), for example, is a vivid metaphor for the mortal body, which was "adopted by Jews and early Christians who wrote in Greek" (page 225). As examples of these two classes, Aune cites (page 313, notes 57, 58) Philo and Paul. Paul may certainly be termed a *Christian writer* but is he not also a Jew?

Stanley K. Stowers caveats himself into meaningless assertions about the "Divide," by stating (page 102) that Pauline Christianity "might in many respects have more in common with Hellenistic philosophies than with the traditional religions based in the landed aristocracies of Rome, Greece and Judea." *Might* is the same as *might not*. One suspects this conclusion has been tailored to fit Stowers' essay into the theme of the book. But why bother? Stowers earlier has said (page 100), "Even though Christianity [and what is that?] did not derive from philosophy in any direct way, but from Judaism, it shared the structural features that made it philosophy-like." My mother-in-law's apple pie is not a cherry pie but it sure is cherry pie-like.

Dale B. Martin faults (page 29) Martin Hengle for having concluded that the Jewish-Hellenistic dichotomy is inevitable as an analytical exercise. But it is, unless "Hellenism" is taken to mean something like *The Dominant Culture* and Judaism is taken to mean merely *an aspect of the Dominant Culture*.

Other contributors also strain against the old dichotomy but finally succumb to it. Loveday Alexander, drawing comparisons between Paul's Corinthian correspondence and contemporary philosophical schools, wants to conclude (page 126) "the categories 'Jewish' and 'Hellenistic' seem to be more or less irrelevant." More? or less? Which is it? Anyway, Alexander finally concedes there were, for Paul, "parallel systems" (page 126) and that between the two "the cultural authorities that Paul appeals to would be sufficient to identify him as 'Jewish' " (page 127).

Philip S. Alexander examines the way in which certain ancient and medieval Christian interpreters perceived Greek influences to be dangerous to theology and thus countered them. But as to the period in question, P. Alexander finds (page 70) there existed analogies between "Greek and Jewish society." Alexander also deduces (page 71) "it was impossible for the rabbis to be Hellenized in any strict sense." If you have "Greek" society in column A and Jewish society in column B together with un-Hellenized rabbis, you have a Jewish-Hellenistic dichotomy.

After creatively comparing and contrasting Josephus and Paul, John M.G. Barclay acknowledges (page 163) Paul continued to employ the categories we are invited to discard; Paul's converts are "still properly labeled Jews and Greeks." Barclay adjusts this terminology ("Greek or non-Greek") just as Paul did but the dichotomy remains. John T. Fitzgerald draws attention to certain motifs developed in "Hellenistic politics" (page 244) which are associated with reconciliation. Fitzgerald thinks (page 242 f.) Paul took over and reworked these motifs, fitting them into his own system. Fitzgerald acknowledges along the way that "certain strong affinities between the Israelite and the Greek traditions should not be denied" (page 317 note 14). If you have both an Israelite and a Greek tradition, you have a dichotomy.

The old Hellenistic-Jewish "Divide" resists the garrote. Why? Because the dichotomy is serviceable. It will continue to be a robust analytical construct because it works. It works even in this volume, which is dedicated to its demise.

APOSTOLIC SPHINX

The Galatians Debate: Contemporary Issues in Rhetorical and Historical Interpretation, Nanos, Mark D, editor, Peabody MA: Hendrickson Publishers, 2002

The Apostle Paul exited this life in a pelage of enigma. We want to figure him out and we want help. We want undaunted scholarship to lay a wreath of syllogisms upon his grave. Our wish has been granted. Across the generations, the wreaths have crowded upon one another. But except for the plastic ones (ironically, more durable), each will wither, leaving room for a newer arrangement, designed with an eye on contemporary tastes and trends.

These essays (some more than thirty years old, almost all collected from scholarly publications) are inventive and diverse treatments gathered under three (arbitrary?) headings. Pauline Rhetoric, Pauline Autobiography and the Situation in Galatia. Some conclusions are plausible. Some not.

What is Paul's letter to the Galatian churches all about? After two thousand years of reflection, the definitive answer is: *we cannot be sure*. This collection, with its 23 essays from 22 scholars, indicates why. Paul's literary, rhetorical and apologetic intentions as well as the events that occasioned the letter and the point(s) of view of the intended recipients are unknowable in a definitive or measurable sense.

Does this mean Nanos (who furnishes two articles of his own) and the other contributors are wasting their time? No. Each of these essays is thoughtful and can be used profitably where Paul's letter is made the subject of inquiry and where diverse points of view are to be considered. There are fundamental questions here as well as proposals that stand in dubious isolation from previous scholarship. Among the contributors who raise basic issues are C. Joachim Classen and John M.G. Barclay.

Classen (writing in 2000) fires cannon across the bow of the rhetorical-analytical frigate, which has been sailing with favorable winds just off the coast of Anatolia for the past twenty-five or thirty years. Classen is firing for effect. He asserts (p.105) the classification of a document and its components neither illuminates the context, which gave rise to the document or clarifies how its components function. Classen argues (p.111) that rhetoric is just another term for oratory and points out (p.105) that "a letter cannot be expected to have the structure of a speech." Worse. The classification of letters "does not assist one in understanding the letter's intentions or any of its details." (p.109) Classen faults Hans Deter Betz (who has contributed a 1975 essay to this volume) for not paying sufficient attention to the distinction between oratory and epistolography (p.98) and for imposing a rhetorical outline upon Galatians without arguing the merits of the selected structural components (Pp.109-110). Betz is also taken to task for ignoring prior applications of rhetorical analysis (Pp. 96, 98-99), especially Philip Melanchthon's (p. 99-103). Classen wonders (p. 97) why Betz limited his study to ancient rhetorical categories. Although an earlier version of Classen's essay appeared in 1993, no direct responses to Classen can be found in this volume. The editor has provided a helpful introductory summary but this is no substitute for actual disputation. Classen's essay is exceptional for this reason. His efforts deserved a direct response.

An absence of genuine debate in this volume may be seen in the contribution of Troy Martin, who apparently has something to debate with J. Louis Martyn - but not in this book. Each scholar appears here but only in reprinted form. In his reproduced 1995 essay, T. Martin argues that the Galatians blamed Paul for their necessary return to paganism because Paul had failed to explain to them the circumcision requirement; this obligation, Martin says, had subsequently been clarified by missionary-agitators, who had followed Paul into the region. Of this proposal,

J.L. Martyn, in his Anchor Bible Commentary (**Galatians**, Doubleday, 1997) commented (page 21, note 26) that T. Martin "has advanced a rhetorical thesis that is so fanciful as to have the effect of suggesting a moratorium of some length in this branch of research." This is the kind of remark, perhaps written at 2 AM, which ought to have been stricken in the light of day.

It is now Martin on Martyn, *mano a mano*. Although T. Martin does not use the opportunity presented by this volume to respond, he does take his revenge (122 *Journal of Biblical Literature* 1 [Spring, 2003], 111-125). Overlooking volume after volume and page after page of J.L. Martyn's published comments on Galatians, T. Martin focuses on a reported oral discussion at a 2000 Society of Biblical Literature section discussion, so as to have J.L. Martyn confess he "doesn't know" what to make of Gal 3:28. Gotcha. I guess.

J.M.G. Barclay, in a 1987 essay reproduced here, argues for caution in *mirror-reading* Paul's letter. Barclay is worried about "the distorting effects of polemic" (p. 369), which may have lead Paul "to caricature his opponents, especially in describing their motivations" (p. 369). Barclay insists (p. 367) that reconstructing the arguments of "the other side" in Galatians is a "difficult and delicate" exercise, which is nevertheless "essential" although "extremely problematic."

Does Barclay leave his readers as people most to be pitied and without hope? Nope. The interpretive dangers of "undue selectivity" and "over-interpretation" of Paul's statements (p. 372) may be met by a cautionary methodology, if "appropriate criteria" are employed (p. 376). Barclay's criteria include (p. 376, ff.) a classification of Paul's "utterances" (assertions? denials? commands? prohibitions?) plus an attempt to tease out of the text such matters as Paul's "tone." Barclay also wants the critic to consider whether Paul's comments are clear, expressive of familiar or unfamiliar motifs, and frequently or infrequently found elsewhere in the letters. Finally, Barclay want to determine whether Paul's "attacks" are "historically plausible," that is, whether what we know of "men [sic] and movements" of Paul's day is reflected in Paul's statements. Barclay includes (p. 377) this arresting thought: "If our results are anachronistic or historically implausible, we will be obliged to start again."

Start what again?

Barclay's suggestions highlight the circularity of every attempt to understand the situation in Galatia: we have Paul's statements and from them we infer conditions "on the ground" and then decide what Paul's statements mean. But is the historian of Paul's letter any differently positioned that any other historian? Isn't all history circular as to the interplay between facts and their significance? It seems to me the task of the historian is not to record but to evaluate. Otherwise, how can one know what to record? E.H. Carr makes this point by reminding that uncounted thousands of individuals have crossed the Rubicon. These are the facts. But the crossing by Caesar is probably the one crossing we must take notice of. (See E.H Carr, **What is History**, [Random House, 1961] page 9).

If history always comes to us refracted through the mind of the historian, then history is *made* by none other than the historian. History is not about what is over and done with but rather is about the present and its needs. This may help explain why the historian, in the guise of poet or prophet, often got into trouble back in the day.

And so, Barclay's caution is fine for Barclay--but not for J. Louis Martyn, who has contributed a 1985 essay, much supplemented in recent years, which has culminated in his previously mentioned commentary (**Galatians,** Doubleday 1997). In his commentary, Martyn has created hypothetical "sermons." This is taking *mirror reading* about as far as can be. Martyn proposes that the sermons he himself has invented are similar to those sermons which must have been composed and delivered in Galatia (the area around Ankara) by Christian Jewish "teachers." These "teachers" allegedly followed Paul into Galatia, and, according to Martyn, wanted to supplement for the Galatian believers the misleading inadequacies they perceived in Paul. Barclay, not surprisingly, found fault (p. 378) with this approach even before Martyn used it to full effect in his commentary. One of Martyn's sermonic inventions, reproduced here (pp. 358-61), demonstrates that, just as in quantum physics, the past can be as unpredictable as the future.

No doubt, future scholars will chase down several of these **Galatians Debate** proposals with the instincts of beagles. Until then, you can read the arguments and judge for yourself. Is Paul in Galatia confronting concrete charges concerning his apostolate, as Martyn proposes? Not so, according to Johan S. Vos (p.180). Is it the case that for Paul "justification through faith" and "covenantal nomism" are "in direct antithesis to each other," as James D.G. Dunn suggests (p. 234)? Do you think "from its inception, the Christian movement admitted Gentiles without demanding that they be circumcised and observe the law," as Paula Fredriksen asserts (p. 255)? Or did Peter in Antioch "demand circumcision" of Gentiles as Philip F. Esler has concluded (p. 281)? On the other hand, might Peter in Antioch have engaged in "obsequious behavior" when he "withdrew from these mixed meals" as Mark Nanos says (p. 317)? Or (door number three, or are we back to door two?) was Peter in Antioch actually "passive-aggressive," somehow compelling the Gentile believers, by withdrawing from them, as Fredriksen concludes (p. 258)? Or is it probable that Peter and "Jewish Christians in Judea were stimulated by Zealotic pressures into a nomistic campaign among their fellow Christians," as Robert Jewett argues (p. 340)? Or was Paul contending in Galatia not with other Christian missionaries but with a "Jewish countermission," as uncovered by Nikolaus Walter (p. 362)? Were there "circumcised people in Galatia who were advocating circumcision of Gentiles not for the purpose of keeping the law but for the purpose of avoiding persecution," as Dieter Mitternacht asserts (p. 409)?

Who prevailed in Galatia? Were Paul's opponents "very successful" in convincing the Galatians "to obey the Torah and adopt a Jewish way of life," as B.C. Lategan maintains (p. 395)? Or, did the Galatians whom Paul addresses become "members of Christ-believing subgroups within larger Jewish communities" who see Paul as "a Torah-observant Jew," as Nanos would have it (p. 405)?

One or two of these suggestions are as plausible as the notion that Paul's antagonists in Galatia were not theological contortionists at all but victims of Paul's earlier persecution. This is my own suggestion ("Paul and the Victims of His Persecution: The Opponents in Galatia," Biblical Theology Bulletin, 32:4, page 182). Its weak points have received two or three coats of Kevlar, like all the other suggestions. It has been put forward with the idea that we should try to keep the situation real. Paul's Celtic converts probably had their noses firmly pressed against the nether side of the Iron Age; they would have had as much fondness for knife wielding circumcisers as John Paul II did for Jean Paul Sartre.

Few of these contributions have taken into account the leading Pauline historians of the past: For a ready summary of these older results consult the critical essays in **The Writings of St. Paul**, edited by Wayne Meeks (Norton 1972). Meeks' own concluding essay, "The Christian Proteus," reminds us of the shape-changing aspect of Paul, a *daimon* who questions us just when we think we are questioning him.

None of us is likely ever to figure Paul out. This is due to the intensity of his rhetoric, the mutual inconsistency of many of his conceptions, and to the large role his mostly muted adversaries have played in shaping his literary legacy. Meeks correctly emphasized all of this.

Paul remains beyond us primarily because his letters are read as Scripture. One must fail as a matter of course at a complete understanding of Scripture. But we may obtain a serendipitous and fragmentary rapport with the message carried by the words, a rapport, which grasps and releases the reader as the contours of wisdom, absurdity, curiosity, humility, self-regard, grief and exaltation effervesce within us from moment to moment.

STRONGER LESSONS

Have you learn'd lessons only of those who admired you?

and were tender with you, and stood aside for you?

Have you not learn'd great lessons from those who

reject you, and brace themselves against you? or who

Treat you with contempt or dispute the passage with you?

Walt Whitman

Sands at Seventy
Leaves of Grass

YOU WANT ME TO CUT OFF . . . *WHAT*?

Cutting Too Close for Comfort: Paul's Letter to the Galatians in its Anatolian Cultic Context. Susan M. Elliott. Journal for the Study of the New Testament Supplement Series 248. London/New York: Continuum, 2003.

Circumcision is to castration as a nose ring is to a lobotomy. It would be hard to confuse one with the other. Yet in **Cutting Too Close for Comfort: Paul's Letter to the Galatians in its Anatolian Cultic Context**, Susan Elliott asks us to believe Paul's ancient Celtic converts would have said circumcision but thought castration. At the beginning of this book, Elliott lays her cards on the table: "Paul's concern about circumcision does not originate from an antipathy toward the Law but from an antipathy toward the cult of the Mother of the Gods and an abhorrence of self-castration" (page 13). Well, if Paul maintained an "abhorrence of self-castration," why would not also the Celts of Galatia? And if they did not find self-castration repellant, how do we know they did not? Toward the end, Elliott concludes (p. 332), "'Flesh' is the flesh of ritual, circumcision or castration." Circumcision *or* castration? If they ask you at the tattoo parlor, "want a nose ring or a lobotomy?" how would you answer?

Circumcision and castration are not easily confused and I find unproven Elliott's argument to the contrary. It cannot be proved in this book, anyway, because, in a book whose thesis demands interpretation of the actual statements in Paul's letter, we are not given exegesis but a proposition and extra-textual data in its support. This data, which Elliott designates (page 119) as "evidence," may prove some things but not others. The data may prove, for example, the prevalence of goddess worship across the Roman Empire. But the data does not prove circumcision is likely to lead to castration. This could only be shown if Elliott had demonstrated why Paul made certain statements in his letter with certain presumed readers in mind. To do that, the text of the letter itself must be examined. But in this book it is not.

Absent exegesis, the reader is left to test the plausibility of the proposed thesis and the data offered in its support. Is it plausible, as Elliott argues, that Paul would have equated circumcision and castration in the Sarah-Hagar analogy of Galatians 4 or in the flesh-spirit dichotomy of Galatians 3? Is it plausible the Celts would have understood him to be doing this? Does the offered data support the thesis? Is it plausible that the *galli* (temple priests) themselves would have reasoned that *either* circumcision *or* castration would be sufficient devotion to Ishtar or Cybele or Demeter, Venus/Aphrodite, Artemis/Diana, or Bellona? These questions, raised by the flow of Elliott's argument, are answered negatively because a positive answer fails the plausibility test.

But lots of stuff happens that is not plausible. So, what can be said about the actual rituals practiced in those *Mountain Mother* temples in Anatolia and throughout the Mediterranean basin? Did all these goddesses require castration? We just don't know. Before we add, "and we just don't care," we note that Elliott argues we should care because Paul cared. But did he? Did anyone care except those *galli*? And what were they up to anyway?

Elliott places (page 167) the self-castrated *galli* in "an interstitial position." If this is not a pun, it should be. The interstitial, that is, the castrated position, is described in a lengthy quotation from Lucian of Samosata. But Lucian has been criticized in some quarters for his lack of objectivity and a bias against none other than the *Galatians* (the *galli*?). There are also citations from Ovid, Pliny the Elder (*Historia Naturalis*), Juvenal and Plutarch, each of whom the author presents as describing self-circumcisions. All of these descriptions are then said (page 162) to have in common "the pattern of self-castration in a state of goddess induced *mania* and subsequent change of clothing . . . ." Elliott concedes (page 163) "Exactly what was severed is not clear". After one hundred and sixty two pages, that is conceding a lot, for it means we do not know what the "something" is that was cut away. Reading "castration" whenever she finds "circumcision" in Paul, Elliott is imposing a rather rigid and artificial consistency on the writer of those urgent, pesky missives.

If someone is going to argue that, for Paul, circumcision and castration were associated, the reader may want a closer examination of what Paul has to say. Before we take up the texts in Galatians where Paul actually mentions "circumcision," I shall permit myself a (hopefully) clarifying aside.

The usual English terminology used to translate Paul here (circumcised / uncircumcised) does of course convey a before-and-after parallel aspect, But there is no parallelism in Paul's Greek. For this reason, this reviewer has opted to translate *peritomês* and *acrobustia* as open tipped and close tipped in Gal 2:7 and 5:6. It is hoped that avoidance of the incessant employment of (un-) circumcision terminology may assist in conveying a graphic - that is, a visual - impact inherent in the ritual of circumcision as contrasted with the practice (?) of castration. To put this another way, the visualization of male genitalia is crucial to the evaluation of Elliott's argument. Paul is talking about the penis prior to and then subsequent to the removal of at least a portion of the foreskin. But Elliott, on the other hand, suggests that the ritual of *circumcision* prompted Paul's Celtic audience to consider not only the excision of some portion of the prepuce but also *the removal of the testicles* as well. This is a dramatically different visualization of "circumcision." Here follows, then, a consideration of the texts of Galatians, where "circumcision" is actually mentioned, with this question rattling around in the (male) readers mind: *you want me to cut off . . . what?*

Gal 2:3: "*But not even Titus, a Greek who was with me, was required to be circumcised*"

This is all Paul has to say about Titus and circumcision. But he does continue, interestingly, as follows: "*As for the leaders, so called—what they actually are I have no way of knowing since God's face is hidden from mankind—these 'leaders' required nothing of me, seeing the obvious: that the Message to the closed-tipped had been entrusted to me, just as to Peter the open-tipped. For the One who empowered Peter into a mission to the open tipped, energized me as well—to gentiles. Seeing this favor that had been entrusted to me, James and Cephas and John, being the Old Guard, formally shook hands with me and with Barnabas, we to gentiles but they to the open tipped"* (Gal 2:6-9).

Undoubtedly, Paul distinguished Gentiles from Jews based on the phenomenon of circumcision. But Elliott says nothing at all about this text because circumcision, as practiced exclusively among Jews, is not a factor in her thesis. Nevertheless, this rite, as practiced by Jews upon Jews, is a concern in Paul's letter.

Gal 2:11-12: *"But after Peter came to Antioch, I got in his face because he stood condemned. For before some from James arrived, he would eat with gentiles. But when they came, he hesitated. And then he held back, fearing those of the open-tipped-only faction."*

Once again, Paul distinguishes Gentiles and Jews by reference to the cutting ritual of circumcision. One would think here, in a Gentile context, there might be some hint of support for Elliott's thesis that Paul was worried that circumcision could lead to castration. But nothing like that can be found directly in the text.

Gal 5:2-3: *"I, Paul, formally certify to you that for anyone who gets himself circumcised, the Messiah is not effective. I testify once again: every circumcised man is obliged to give effect to the whole law."*

Paul is drawing a distinction between circumcision, as a cultic legal requirement, and the apocalyptic arrival of the Messiah, which has wiped away the circumcision obligation. This dense argument is made more obtuse, because Paul resorted to legal jargon to assert the invalidity of a legal obligation, and then asserted, quite illogically, that observance of Torah in every detail was mandated for anyone who intended to adopt a portion of it. But there is no explicit statement by Paul that he has castration in mind. Nor does the text suggest that he is concerned his Celtic converts will somehow confuse the two procedures, or, adopting the one they will be drawn to adopt the other.

Gal 5:6: *"In Christ, neither an open tip nor a closed tip is of any importance."*

Elliott argues that Galatians 5:6 shows Paul was resisting the Mountain Mother's alleged requirement that the men who serve her undergo ether circumcision *or* castration. But is it possible to find support in this statement for the notion that Paul is concerned that his converts, allegedly influenced by the *galli*, are likely to castrate themselves? This reviewer finds Elliott unpersuasive here. Since Paul is completely silent about an association between circumcision and castration, there is nothing here to support the thesis that the *galli*, self-castrating temple priests, are the targets of Paul's polemic in Galatians.

Paul is completely silent in his own letter about the extent to which castration may have been related to his writing about circumcision. An argument from silence is more about silence than about an argument. In that regard, Elliott's book reads more coherently from back to front. That is, the book is constructed like a legal argument, a brief, which is written after conclusions have already been reached and some audience has to be persuaded. In support of the pre-determined conclusions, arguments are then made. This reviewer is left with the impression that Paul's own statements on the subject at hand are not clarified so much as ignored.

On a positive note, **Cutting Too Close for Comfort** draws needed attention to the fact that Paul is addressing Gentile communities living in a Gentile context. These were people Paul himself had recruited into what, retrospectively, we may consider the second wave of converts, that is, Gentiles who has accepted the invitation of Paul and before him, other missionaries to Gentiles, to participate in the scattering of *worldwide* communities celebrating the dawning Messianic age. (The first wave of converts, in my estimation, included people Paul himself had persecuted. Please see, "Paul and the Victims of his Persecution: the Opponents in Galatia," 32 Biblical Theology Bulletin, No. 4, 182-91, 2002; reprinted in this volume, pp 53-92.)

Scholarly responses undoubtedly will acknowledge Elliott's creativity and the emphasis placed on Celtic Anatolia. This emphasis is an important and necessary corrective to the recent, almost exclusive focus upon Jewish influences traced in Paul. Paul himself certainly was subject to such influences but this does not mean many of his intended readers would have been. I believe the value of Elliott's contribution is to invite renewed interest in the Gentile milieu in which Paul conducted his activities; this focus will permit greater specificity about the confluence of issues addressed by Paul in his letter to the churches in Galatia.

"SHOULD I GET TO HEAVEN I WILL BE PRAYING FOR YOU THERE"

Joshua Flood Cook

Cecil V Cook, Sr (1871-1948)
Cecil V Cook, Jr (1913-1970)

Joshua Flood Cook (1834-1912) was born near Bagdad, KY (some 30 miles east of Louisville) on Jan 14, 1834. He died in LaGrange, Missouri in May, 1912. Joshua was the son of **Lucy Flood** (1802-1865) and **William Fredrick ("Billy Dick") Cook** (1802-b/f 1855). William and Lucy Cook's other children were Joseph, Alexander, Mary and Abraham. At age 13, Joshua thought he would become a blacksmith and undertook a three-year apprenticeship (1847-50).

In 1850 young Joshua moved to Missouri and lived for four years with his uncle, the well known Baptist preacher, Noah Flood, which is a name combo that must always have had a tick of humor for the parents, who put it together. In Missouri Joshua went to Fayette High School in Howard County. While attending high school (1850-54), Joshua is said to have also been a school teacher. If true, this suggests that Joshua had been doing his own studying while an apprentice blacksmith in KY. It is also an early indication that Joshua benefited from personal connections in Missouri, connections which would be fruitful in the years to come.

In 1854, Joshua returned to Kentucky and became a student at Georgetown College; he graduated in 1858. In a memoir (**Old Kentucky**, 1908) Joshua wrote that he was licensed to the Baptist ministry while a student at Georgetown. The licensing was promptly followed by Joshua's ordination as a Baptist minister in 1858 at Campbellsburg, KY.

Joshua described himself as "homeless" when he went to Georgetown College in 1855. He had not lived at home with his parents since at least age 16 when he went to

Missouri. Joshua has also written that he spent his college vacations visiting in the homes of his classmates rather than with his own family. Joshua reported in his 1908 memoir that his childhood home broke up upon his father's death and his mother's subsequent 1855 marriage to Thomas Brewer. It is not known whether Joshua might have been unwelcome in Thomas Brewer's home or whether, already twenty-one in 1855, he had simply concluded he was old enough to manage without a home.

On Nov. 4, 1858, Joshua married **Susan Goode Farmer** (1838-1890). Sue Farmer was born August 8, 1838 in Kentucky and died in Missouri on May 10, 1890. She was the namesake of her grandmother, **Susan Goode** (1783-1864), who had been born in the Skinquarter section of Chesterfield County, Virginia, the daughter of a locally well known and dissenting Baptist preacher, the excitable **John Goode** (1739-1792). (It was said of John Goode by a contemporary, William Hickman, that when John spoke of his religious convictions, *"he got so warm he scarcely would sit on his saddle."*)

Susan's mother, **Katherine Spencer Hawkins Farmer** (1814-1851) died when Sue was thirteen. Little Susie was left with the care of four brothers, one of whom, Joseph, was but one year old when their mother Katherine died. Another brother, Willie Farmer (1848-1862), would die in agony from wounds received on the Shiloh battlefield in 1862, fighting for the Confederacy. After Willie's death, Sue wrote to her father **John Goode Farmer** (1808-1871), from Mississippi.

Oh my dear Pa, I cannot <u>cannot</u> realize that my dear brother is dead, that he sleeps the sleep that knows no waking. Shall I not again see him or hear him tell his deep anxiety to get home to loved ones once more. And never no never in this life can I see him. Ah! If there is recognition in heaven! Is this thought filled my dear ma's head, when she sees her dear son free from his torments of earth and walking in God's glory [. . .] I should have given anything in the world to have had him with me in his last moments but God's ways are not as ours. He expressed a *great desire to be brought home after Mr. Cook got there but it was <u>impossible</u>. He could not be moved enough to change his clothes! And no father or sister near - is almost more than I can bear. He sleeps in our church yard so I can visit his resting place every evening with little Ernest, who seems conscious that it is a sacred spot to me, for he comes and places his arms around my neck and says, "Bless Uncle Will in the sky".*

In 1858, Joshua Cook, a newly married, newly minted college graduate and preacher, became chaplain of New Liberty Female College (now defunct), New Liberty, KY. In 1859, at age twenty-five, Joshua was made president of this institution and held that post until the outbreak of the Civil War in 1861.

Susan and Joshua had four children: John Ernest (1860-1926), Lula (1862-1943), William Flood (1868-?) and **Cecil Virgil** (1871-1948). The Rev. John Ernest Cook was born in Kentucky, July 17, 1860; Lula was born in Corinth Mississippi August 27, 1862, William Flood, in LaGrange Missouri, Feb 2, 1868; **Cecil Virgil** (1871-1948) was also born in LaGrange, Dec. 10, 1871.

In 1861, J.F. Cook left New Liberty College and moved his family to Summit, Mississippi, where he became a school teacher and chaplain to Confederate Army troops. During the war, Joshua bought farmland in Mississippi, about two hundred miles north of New Orleans. The disposition of this property has not yet been traced. Nor is it known how Joshua and Sue Cook financed this purchase or whether they conducted agricultural activities and worked slaves on this land. In 1865, Joshua and Susan returned to KY, where he assumed the pastorate of the Baptist church at Eminence, KY.

On Sept. 7, 1865, Joshua Cook once again was chosen to be president of a college, this being a co-educational school then known as the LaGrange Male and Female Seminary. The college was located in LaGrange, MO, a small town on the banks of the Mississippi River about 100 miles north of St. Louis. Joshua was thirty-two. In 1868, Joshua was awarded an honorary doctorate

(LL.D.) from Baylor University, Waco, TX. He was ever after referred to as Doctor J.F. Cook.

Joshua held the presidency of LaGrange College for thirty years. In the twentieth century, after Joshua had passed from the scene, the college relocated to nearby Hannibal, MO and became Hannibal-LaGrange College.

In 1912 (the year of his death) Joshua reminisced about how difficult was his struggle to obtain an education. "I live in a dream from early boyhood," he wrote to his son Cecil, "Almost broke myself down trying to get an education. They [thought?] once they would have to send me to an asylum - but I rallied." This curious statement is unaccompanied by any clarifying facts, but suggests an early and overt anxiety to acquire what was not readily available to a farmer's son in the middle of the nineteenth century: schooling. Somehow, Joshua pulled it off.

In 1858 he not only graduated from college, but was invited to deliver a graduation speech. The original document, preserved and reproduced by proud descendents, reflects the florid oratorical style of its time and also indicates Joshua's solid command of the written and spoken word. Joshua took as his subject a well known Baptist Missionary. This choice probably reflects Joshua's exposure to books in the Missouri home of his uncle, the Rev. Noah Flood, whose library no doubt included an emphasis upon Baptist history and traditions. A short excerpt from Joshua's 1858 graduation address:

> *"Among the brave, the great, the good of our country, whose names are worthy to be transmitted to posterity, stately column or immortalizing song will never guard the memory of a nobler spirit than Adoniram Judson. For sublime, heroic action, for noble, pure Christian philanthropy, for devoted love to every human creature, he may justly challenge comparison with any that have lived. He knew not self, he felt not his own woes - he lived for others."*

Joshua Flood Cook

Joshua Cook's own library grew throughout his life and contained a number of volumes, which have made their way on to the shelves of his children, grandsons, and great grandchildren. J. F. Cook cherished his books. At age seventy, he acquired a copy of **Outlines of Medieval and Modern History**, by J.V.N. Myers (Boston: Gynn & Company 1903) which he loaned to someone and which he inscribed, "When done with this, return immediately to J.F. Cook, LaGrange, MO." J.F. got his book back.

Joshua Cook's 30-year tenure (1866-96) at LaGrange College was viewed as a success by contemporaries. He was said to have assumed charge and then saved the school, when it had but a single dilapidated building, no money in the bank and a debt burden of $10,000, a sum equivalent to at least fifty times that amount by the standards of today. Reflecting on his tenure in a letter to son Cecil, J.F. Cook recalled in 1912 how hard the task was. "The thirty years here [LaGrange] were too much. No living soul knows what I went through those years. Wonder I am living and that I have any mind."

The arrangement Joshua made with the trustees at the 1866 beginning was to lease the college from them for a ten-year term, raise the needed funds and conduct an educational program as specified by the charter and the policies laid down by the trustees. Joshua, as lessee of the College, could keep any amount raised above that needed for college expenses. This seems to have been the agreement for three consecutive ten-year leases, from 1866 to 1896.

The college trustees expected the enforcement of strict standards and President Cook delivered. Applicants were required to meet with an admissions committee. Parents as well as prospective students were advised of the behavioral standards required of the students.

An "Abstract of College Laws" dating from J.F. Cook's tenure, contained the following provisions:

Every student shall attend the daily devotional exercises in the college chapel, also, public worship on the

Lord's day, at such churches as the parent or guardian may designate.

Students will not be permitted to be absent from their rooms after 7 o'clock at night without leave, except to attend religious service, or the literary societies connected with the college.

No student will be permitted to leave the city on any pretext whatever, during his or her connection with the college, without previous permission from the president or some member of the faculty.

No student shall carry deadly weapons, or attend any exhibition having an immoral tendency, nor frequent any bar-room or tippling house.

Students in the male and female departments are to have no communications, either verbal or written, further than true politeness requires.

An 1872 advertisement for the college in the LaGrange *Democrat* included the following statement: "Moral and religious influences here are superior, students being unexposed to the vices and temptations of larger cities. One hundred and seventy-five dollars will pay the tuition for the college year. Our students are living with the best of families, not in mess halls. The graduates of this institution are as good as any other college in the state."

Soon after moving to LaGrange, Joshua and Sue Cook built a 14-room brick mansion at the edge of the college campus. They moved into it in 1868. Their residence "on the hill" was the focal point of fund raising and social activities for the college. At graduation, an elaborate reception, a "levee," would be conducted at the President's home. J.F. Cook also organized an alumni association and encouraged alumni to support the school.

During all of the years at LaGrange, Sue Cook was helpfully at Joshua's side. The mother of four children, she nevertheless fulfilled the social requirements that fell to the spouse of a college president. Sue Farmer Cook also continued to look after her Farmer siblings in Kentucky, whom she had helped care for after their mother had died young. Following her move to Missouri, Sue influenced her siblings to join her and Joshua there. The 1870 Lewis County Missouri census reports the Cook household contained J F Cook, age 36, Sue G, 29, Ernest, 10, "Lulu"[Lula], 7, and Willie 2; there is also Lucius Farmer, 21, Sue's brother and himself a student at the college. There is also Brinkman Lewis 17, a student. The household also included Sarah Fisher, 16, Black, a "domestic servant," born in Kentucky. Sue's youngest brother, Joseph, became a professor at LaGrange College. Ellery Farmer, the Farmer family genealogist, concluded that Sue influenced virtually all of her siblings to move from Kentucky to Missouri.

In 1887, J.F. Cook gave a twenty-year report to the trustee and announced he had raised and expended over $15,000 for debt retirement and building improvements. The college, he said, had assets greater than indebtedness. During the 1880's, college enrollment exceeded the University of Missouri and the college was widely acknowledged for its co-educational focus. One may surmise that Sue Cook was a stimulus and advocate for the education of women. Daughter Lula attended and graduated from LaGrange College.

While in charge of the college, J.F. Cook exercised his calling as a Baptist minister. For at least fourteen years he was pastor of Dover Baptist church in Pike County, Missouri. The church building, constructed in 1862, still stands: Route D, Calumet Township. In May, 1890, a delegation from this congregation attended the funeral of Susan Cook, who had died on LaGrange College commencement day.

Susan Cook was the subject of a lengthy obituary in the LaGrange *Democrat*, which pointed out her life-long active interest in the local Baptist Church, including her long incumbency as Sunday School teacher of the youngest class. She also raised funds for the completion of a new "church house." Sue's own funeral was the first to take place in the completed building.

Susan Goode Farmer Cook

An unspecified lingering, painful illness preceded Susan Cook's death. Near the end Sue gave directions for her funeral, which included a request that her Sunday School class "attend the funeral in a body and the members of it throw into her open grave flowers of their own cutting and arranging." This was done. The newspaper observed: *"The class, made up of the youngest children, had reserved seats, each little one bearing flowers of his or her own gathering. Huddled in their select corner the tear-stained, motherless brood presented one of the most touching features of the funeral procession."*

Sue Cook's death was a severe blow to the morale of her husband. President Joshua Flood Cook, the public man, acknowledged this. In August, 1890, two short months after Sue Cook's death, J.F. Cook, was observed to be "somewhat depressed" when he attended the Wyaconda Baptist Association's annual meeting; he mentioned that he might resign from the school. But the Association, as partners with him through the trustees of the college, offered Joshua a lifetime contract and over-pledged funds for needed improvements. He returned home, it was reported, "inspired, and determined to make renewal efforts and think no more of surrendering this charge until relieved by physical infirmity."

In 1893 a near tragedy at the college became an episode worthy of the Marx brothers. While J.F. was in New Orleans, flames spread by chimney sparks set fire to the roof of one of the main college buildings. Thanks to the quick action of neighbors, no lasting damage was done. But where was the LaGrange fire department? "The tardiness of the fire department was accounted for by the fact that a pair of very small mules hitched to the truck, in addition to the apparatus, had to haul about a dozen able-bodied men to the top of the hill." The newspaper, which reported the presence of the "very small mules," does not state whether in future, larger mules would be harnessed to the fire wagon or whether firemen would be asked to run to fires that were uphill from the firehouse.

J.F. Cook continued at LaGrange College for a full thirty years, resigning in 1896. He then promptly assumed the presidency of Webb City College, Webb City, MO, and continued there until his final retirement in 1900. In that year Joshua returned to LaGrange and lived there until his death in 1912.

Joshua was married three times: his first wife, as stated, was **Susan Goode Farmer** (1838-1890); they wed on Nov. 4, 1858. In May 1891, a year after Sue's death, Joshua married Bessie Hughes of Saline County, Missouri. They had no children. Bessie died of tuberculosis on May 8, 1894, almost four years to the day after the death of Joshua's first wife. In 1895, Joshua married Drusilla Hirons (?-Nov 12, 1962). They became the parents, in 1900, of Howard Elliott Cook; Joshua was then sixty-six years old. Howard Cook fought in World War II; he was captured on Wake Island in 1941 and spent three years as a Japanese prisoner of war, apparently held in Shanghai. Suffering from lingering traumatic stress after the war, Howard required care the rest of his days. He lived in Florida with his mother Drusilla until his death. Both Howard and Drusilla ("Aunt Drusie") are buried beside J. F. Cook, in LaGrange, Missouri.

"OLD KENTUCKY"

In 1908 J. F. Cook published a book of reminiscences which he titled **Old Kentucky**. Much of the information we have about Joshua and his immediate family has been taken from this book, which is a paean to the Kentucky of Joshua's youth, as J.F. recalled, in his eighth decade. Undoubtedly, Joshua intended his book, sprinkled with opinion and the occasional Baptist minister's joke or pun, to be received as a serious and valuable contribution to the annals of his home state. He dedicated his book to "Colonel Reuben T. Durrett, Scholar, Historian, Founder of the Filson Club," in Louisville, KY, The Filson Club continues to be a noted repository of Kentucky history and documentation. Durrett contributed a chapter to J.F.'s book, entitled *"Kentucky, Her History and Her People."* Joshua sought and received permission from President Theodore Roosevelt to include a selection of Roosevelt's writings in the volume, which appear in a chapter entitled *"Kentuckians and Bordermen."*

A third contributor to Joshua's volume was then Congressman and future Speaker of the House of Representatives, Champ Clark of Missouri. For three years J.F. Cook's oldest son, John Ernest Cook (July 7, 1860-Dec 2, 1926), had been Champ Clark's law partner in Bowling Green, MO.

Joshua has written in **Old Kentucky** (pages 135, 136, 137) that he grew up in Shelby County KY, surrounded by all of his grandparents and most of their children. Joshua remembered his boyhood with a nostalgic glow, notable even for a sentimental old man.

"Every house was near a fine spring, and around them grew magnificent forests. Such forests I have seen no where else between ocean and ocean . . . In those days there were trees standing with the marks made on them by the claws of bears, and grandfather has pointed out to me different trees where he had killed bears after he settled there. . . I see the old house as I saw it when a child. The first house or cabin had been turned into a hen house; the house that was new when I was born was of hewed logs, two rooms. The upstairs of the house was all one room, where we boys slept and we were well and happy. . . . Grandfather owned all the land and had enough to divide and give homes to a large family of children. We always had good gardens, abundance of milk, and butter and poultry. Nearly every home had its bees, and when the family desired more honey, they could go out in the woods and cut down a bee tree. . . . What more to be desired then these old time people had?"

The elderly Joshua recalled his childhood with an extravagant reverie that would do credit to the troubadours who touted Robin Hood and Jolly Old England. Joshua wrote (page 138) that hardly a boy in the neighborhood failed to grow up to less than six feet tall "rugged, hardy splendid men, and girls into beautiful women." Joshua, himself six feet tall, seems to have enjoyed good health, despite a bout with typhoid fever in 1844, when he was ten years old (page 133). Joshua lived to be seventy eight.

Devout from an early age, Joshua took his zeal in the Baptist, frontier style. "Before I was thirteen years old, I was lead to Christ and never, from that day to this [1846-1908] have I ever purposely done anything to dishonor my profession." By "profession" Joshua is taken to mean not his secular career as a college administrator or even his calling as a Baptist Minister, but his "profession" of faith in Jesus, to which he committed himself as a boy of twelve.

Joshua's paradoxical memories and musings are intriguing and illusive in equal measure. He was twenty-seven years old when the Civil War began. Joshua's mature memories and perspective cover three important epochs: ante-bellum Kentucky and Missouri, the Civil War in the western regions of the South (Mississippi, Kentucky, and Tennessee) and the period of Reconstruction as observed by an energetic and admired educator in small-town Missouri.

Joshua takes care to infuse his memoir with a tranquil and positive aura of gentility. The larger social themes of the period – the national economic life, the transformative employment of electricity and steam power, a massive and bloody civil conflict and the subsequent establishment of a rigid race-conscious caste system, the settlement of the West; all are overlooked. Slavery and its causes and consequences, and civil war, Joshua takes to be difficult episodes which he had the good taste to survive.

Joshua's selective reminiscences transform his memories into soft-toned fancies. He writes (page 159, 162) that General John C. Breckinridge ("the ideal Kentuckian") came to Chaplain J F Cook at a Confederate Camp at Jackson, Mississippi "put his arms around me, and said, 'Cook, we shall never win. We shall all be a set of rag-a-muffins.' I was shocked and surprised and never breathed it to another human being."

Joshua writes (page 159, 158) that Lincoln was "the only man . . . called to the great and seemingly impossible task of leading the nation to the final settlement of the two questions which lead to the war: slavery" and "whether all the states were bound together by a rope of sand or whether they were bound in an indissoluble union." Joshua cites (page 163) his friend Green Clay Smith as "an intimate friend of Mr. Lincoln's, really his pet, and always had free access to him and to the White House. He has told me many incidents that I have never seen published in regard to Mr. Lincoln's private troubles, some of which I could tell but it would probably do no good."

"THE RACE OF HAM"

J.F. Cook's memoir is more than dreamy reminiscences found in the musings of a genial old man. Race and race-consciousness were longstanding obsessions with Joshua. Throughout his reminiscences, he often returns to these themes. Invoking phrenology, that nineteenth century pseudoscientific fad, Joshua writes (page 39) that official Civil War autopsies demonstrate "the negro brain is over five ounces less than that of the white;" moreover, "the percentage of exceptionally small brains is largest among the negroes having but a small percentage of white blood." These *facts* appear to prove to Joshua (page 40) "that the race of Ham has ever had some cloud hanging darkly over it."

Joshua does not speculate about the nature of the "cloud," or the interactions required to introduce "white blood" among African slaves. A greater degree of candor by Joshua, might have better enlightened his readers to learn what he must have known to be true, that there occurred in the "Old Kentucky" of blessed memory the regular assault by white men and boys upon female slaves, both girls and women, who had not the slightest means of protecting themselves.

The nexus between race and sexual union was The Forbidden Subject in the ante-bellum South. Joshua carried this prohibition forward into the twentieth century. Well aware of the taboo, Joshua speaks of racial matters only in terms of superior versus inferior peoples. Joshua invokes white racial superiority to clarify (page 40) the family's traditional interest in owning human beings.

"*By way of explanation, I want to say that my ancestors, all of whom were from Virginia, owned slaves; that I inherited slaves, that I was reared among them; and from childhood I played with them and loved them, and in after years, when they came into my possession, I was as kind and tender to them as if they had been of my own race, and in my whole life never bought or sold one; that I have contributed to their education after they were freed.*"

Following this defensive broadside, delivered forty years after the Civil War, Joshua retreats to the safe haven of abstract musings (page 41): "*Why God, in his providence, permitted this country to make the blunders it did, no human mind can comprehend.*"

Joshua relates (page 46) that his grandfather - whether **Abraham Cook** (1774-1854) or **Joshua Flood** (1772-1850) he does not specify - once offered his slaves their freedom to go to Ohio. But they preferred "to remain in Kentucky - with him and live with him; and they did until some of them died, and others were kindly cared for after his death." The mention of the death of this grandfather suggests that Grandfather Flood is in mind; Abraham Cook moved to Missouri before he died.

According to Cook wills, slaves were owned and also bought and sold by family members. Seth, Joshua's great uncle - the son of Joshua's great grandfather **William Cook** (abt 1730-abt 1790/91) provided in his 1842 will for the sale of a black man, Sandy, who was valued at $100.00. Another of Joshua's great uncles, William Cook, stipulated in his 1816 will that a slave, "Peter should be free on the payment of Fifty Dollars; a balance of two-hundred and fifty dollars which Seth Cook and Abraham Bohannon as agents for Peter had undertaken to pay which is all paid but the aforesaid fifty dollars."

Believing the Civil War was fought to resolve the question of slavery, Joshua also believed (page 46) that the white citizens of Kentucky would have freed their slaves but for a single factor: "constant agitation awakened bad feelings, and the people of Kentucky did not feel like being driven to anything by falsehood and abuse." Joshua implies that the only abuse he knew of that might be connected with slavery was directed against "the [White] people of Kentucky" who were put upon by "constant agitation."

By 1908, Joshua was (page 47) an admirer of abolitionist John Brown. Joshua knew religious fervor when he saw it and so describes John Brown as "that poor old fanatic" who nonetheless "had courage to risk all to carry out his convictions." The compliment to John Brown becomes a segue into another subject: the collective insanity of slavery's opponents. Joshua now condemns Northern anti-slavery sentiment as "a pitch of madness," because "the Bible was not strong enough" for Northerners on the abolition question, the "'madness" being Northern declarations for "an anti-slavery God, an anti-slavery Constitution, and an anti-slavery Bible."

It is little wonder that, according to **Betty Cook** (1918-2000), wife of J F's grandson **Cecil V. Cook, Jr** (1913-1970), Joshua's 1908 memoir was received with chagrin by his son, **Cecil Cook Sr** (1871-1948), and others of the family. For the aged Joshua, looking back on the war from the distance of fifty years, old John Brown and the rest of those pesky Northerners had taken things too far. *"My opinion is that slavery was a dark shadow upon this country; that in nature it could not exist in a republic; and that Providence let this thing be developed so that it could be abolished; and that it has given to the American people a great problem which no man can solve, but which calls for the wisest and most conservative action."*

In all of his remarks about slavery and race, J. F. may be talking about the enslaved past but his eye is on the era of his successful career as an educator. This career coincided with Reconstruction and extended to the cusp of the new century, the so-called "Progressive" era. Joshua retired from the Presidency of LaGrange College in the year the Supreme Court announced (1896) the fiction in *Plessy v. Ferguson* that demeaning and near worthless "separate" government-provided services were, in Constitutional terms, considered "equal." Joshua could have written *Plessy*. Indeed, the very purpose of *Plessy* was to placate the influential and widely held views, which Joshua epitomized in his memoir.

Joshua reminds his readers that he grew up in a time of human slavery but he does not then state clearly how he lived out the rest of his life in a time of apartheid. His ambiguity about slavery as both a family custom and a large historical motif permits Joshua's to adopt a studied ambivalence towards severe post-Civil War White hostility directed against former slaves – hostility that insisted upon the brutal re-segregation of the region. Joshua embraces this ambivalence in the afterglow of his reminiscence. He offers an easy detachment as a substitute for what surely was, during his public career, an endorsement of the vigorous retrenchment, which was under way during the post Civil War generation.

What might be said in Joshua defense? The currents of reaction had to be taken into account by a college President trying to raise money and shoulder all the other tasks necessary for the survival of a segregated Baptist college in Missouri from 1866-1896. Had Joshua been so foolhardy as to distance himself from the retrenchment called "redemption" or "Jim Crow," he could not have had a career at all. Much of J.F. Cook's memoir reads like notes for the fund raising addresses he made to Baptist gatherings in the cities and towns of Missouri in the final four decades of the nineteenth century.

Slavery, Joshua announces in 1908, "developed so that it could be abolished." This is casuistry of the first water. Undeterred, Joshua continues. The presence, he says, in one society of freed Black slaves and defeated White slavers calls for "the wisest" but also the "most conservative action." Joshua's convoluted bromides are the opinions of a White, prestige-conscious stakeholder.

Nothing is said here of beatings, lynchings, or of voting rights prohibitions and other legal restrictions that accompanied the retrenchment, just as Joshua wrote nothing about brutal slave conditions in Kentucky before the war. We find nothing from Joshua about the slave pens of Lexington and Louisville, or about runaways, or the "paterollers" (patrollers) who hunted them down. Nor does

Joshua reminisce about Kentucky's reputation as a prime breeding state for Mississippi field hands and the "fancy girls" who were bred in Kentucky and sold off to the bordellos of New Orleans.

JOHN MURPHY: OPPONENT OF SLAVERY

We have noted Joshua's remark: *"my ancestors, all of whom were from Virginia, owned slaves."* While this may be literally true, there were dissenting voices within the family and even among those members of the family who felt themselves called to a holy vocation. In Kentucky in the early decades of the nineteenth century and especially in the Baptist context (where *calling* is ratified by majority vote of the congregation) those who opposed slavery paid a severe price for their convictions. One of these was Joshua's great uncle, John Murphy (1752-1818). John Murphy (1752-1818) was a Baptist preacher, the son of William Murphy (by 1726-1799) and his first wife, Martha Hodges (?-by 1767). John's father, William Murphy was himself an early Baptist preacher. In 1757, William was baptized in Orange (now Chatham) County, NC, by the notable Shubal Stearns, a "new light" (Baptist) from New England, who brought the principles of religious dissent into Virginia and NC as early as 1755. William Murphy soon became a Baptist preacher and traveled and lived for years the life of a farmer and an itinerant frontier preacher. (For more on the *new light* phenomenon, see the memoir of William Hickman, appended to **All of the Above II.**

John Murphy married Rachel Cook on Feb 8, 1774. Rachel was the daughter of **Margaret Jones** (1734-1797) and **William Cook Jr** (abt 1730-abt 1790/91). This ancient couple were Joshua's great grandparents. Rachel and John Murphy were the aunt and uncle of **William Fredrick Cook,** a son of **Sarah Jones** (1777-1857) and **Abraham Cook** (1774-1854), who was a brother to Rachel. Rachel Cook and John Murphy were, therefore, the great aunt and uncle of Joshua Flood Cook.

No doubt John met Rachel after William and Martha Murphy had re-located their family to the Pigg

River in Southside Virginia, near the home of William and Margaret Cook. John Murphy took an oath of allegiance to the United States of America on August 30, 1777 and was appointed Ensign of Captain Haile's militia company in March, 1779. In Feb 1782, he was a lieutenant in the Washington County NC militia. After the war, John Murphy and Rachel Murphy followed a semi-nomadic career, notable ever for those times of frequent family moves. Various land transactions have John recorded as a resident of Virginia, North Carolina, Tennessee and Kentucky.

John Murphy was baptized by his brother-in-law Isaac Barton on Dec 4, 1790 in NC or Tennessee and became a member of the Bent Creek Baptist Church in Green County, TN. By November 1798, John and Rachel Murphy are found living in Barren County, KY, where they were enrolled as founding members of the Mount Tabor Baptist Church. John was the first clerk of this congregation and was licensed to preach in 1801. Some time after that date, he took up preaching duties in Kentucky, along the Green River.

John's career as a Baptist minister in Kentucky was cut short because of his hostility to slavery. In 1808, John Murphy was "excluded" by the Mount Tabor (Kentucky) Church "on account of his declaring non-fellowship" with the church "for tolerating slavery." The mutual denunciations appear to have ended John Murphy's career as a preacher. Carter Tarrant, himself an anti-slavery Kentucky preacher and one-time pastor of Mount Tabor Church, said of John Murphy, "He was the first minister south of Green river, who publicly opposed slavery." Spencer's **History of Kentucky Baptists From 1769-1885** (1886, Vol I, page 387) which is our source for the Tarrant comment, states of John Murphy, "What became of him after his exclusion from the church, does not appear." Thanks to the careful research of family historians Elizabeth L Nichols (2004) and Alice Murphy Sturgess (1918), John Murphy's views on slavery have been preserved.

From Warren County, KY in 1810, John wrote a letter to "Brothers, friends and acquaintances" in what came to be St Francois County, Missouri (which John Murphy refers to as "Louisiana Territory"). In addition to family news, John made these comments:

"There is considerable dissention among the Baptists and some among other sects about slave holding. For my own part, I prefer to stand opposed to that system, because I fully believe it to be contrary to the law of nature, contrary to sound reason, contrary to good policy, contrary to justice, contrary to republican principles, and above all, because it is in direct opposition to the Scripture directions. Neither does it accord with the principles of humanity."

The earliest publication of this letter seems to have been in 1918. (Alice M Sturgess' pamphlet – see Sources, below.) This was too late for Joshua Cook's 1908 memoir.

The exclusion of any reference to John Murphy points to several other historical phenomena, which are ignored in Joshua's **Old Kentucky.** These elements, which are unremarked by Joshua are: (1) the turmoil among the early nineteenth century (White) Baptists of Kentucky about slave-holding; (2) the presence of dissenters from the slave-holding consensus, within Joshua's' extended family and (3) the silencing by exclusion from membership in the church of those who objected to slavery on moral grounds. All of these features are typified by the aborted pastoral career of Joshua's great uncle, John Murphy. The sad but significant fact is that the system of slave ownership was not generally accepted among (White) Kentucky Baptists until principled people of conscience such as John Murphy, were separated from the local church. The process of exclusion began in the first decade of the 1800s and continued until the 1830s, when a universally enforced consensus carried the day.

"THE DEATH OF COOK AND THE DISORGANIZATION OF THE KU KLUX KLAN WAS A GREAT RELIEF TO MANY"

Just as Joshua's 1908 memoir neglects to remember anything about his great uncle John Murphy, Joshua passed without a word over Reconstruction in Kentucky, and the human costs inflicted upon its victims, on the larger society and even upon his own extended family. In fairness, he was in Missouri during the post-war decades, but J.F.'s large, extended family were yet Kentuckians; they were present and they were players in some of the more sensational and violent local events of those times. Members of his family are found both as victims and as aggressors. On whatever side, they proved quick to resort to the weapons at hand.

Joshua's father William Cook had a brother, Wesley (?-1864), husband of Sarah King (?-1892). Wesley and Sarah were the parents of numerous children: Elizabeth, Amanda, Martin, Zerilda, Addison (1846-Aug 16, 1871), Alexander, Simeon, Cynthia, Smith, Thomas, and Ella. Here follows a record of the murder of Addison Cook:

In 1870 and 1871 there was an organized band of lawless men in [Shelby] county, who operated principally in the northern and northeastern part of the county. The organization was known as the Ku Klux Klan, and members of it whose homes were in the vicinity of Bagdad, Consolation and Jacksonville, were suspected of being the parties who assaulted and beat a colored mail agent, in the early part of 1871, while in his mail car, that was then standing on the railroad track near Benson Station. The local authorities were helpless, for the reason that the people of the vicinity where the outrages occurred were afraid to give information that would lead to the arrest of the guilty parties, knowing that if they did so that the vengeance of the Ku Klux Klan would fall heavily upon them.

After the assault had been made on the negro mail agent, the Government officials took the matter in hand

and a company of U.S. soldiers was sent to Bagdad in the spring of 1871. This company was Troop 1 of the Seventh Cavalry, Capt. Miles W. Keogh, commanding. The company was stationed at Bagdad for several months, when it moved to Shelbyville, into quarters in a brick livery stable that stood then, at 8th and Main streets, owned by Mr. James L. Long. By the way, this company remained in Shelbyville a couple of years and went from here to Lebanon, and from there out West. Out there it was a part of General Custer's command, that was massacred by the Indians, Capt. Keogh and all of his men, as well as Gen. Custer, and many others, being killed.

It was while the soldiers were at Bagdad that a tragedy occurred within a half-mile of that town, and the trial of the defendant, on a charge of murder, was one of the most interesting and hard-fought in the history of the county. The defendant in the case was Hiram Bohannon, a reputable citizen, and the man whom he killed was Addison Cook, a reckless dare-devil, and the alleged leader of the Ku Klux Klan. There had been hard feelings between the men for some time, for the reason that some one had told Cook that Bohannon had said that he (Cook) had proposed to the Government to give the Klan away for $20,000, and Cook had threatened to kill Bohannon, on numerous occasions. On the morning of August 15th, 1871, Bohannon went to a point about half-way between Bagdad and Consolation, with his shotgun, loaded with buckshot, and waited for Cook, whom he knew would go that morning from Consolation to Bagdad. There were no eye-witnesses to the killing, but the circumstantial evidence that Bohannon had killed Cook was strong, and he never denied it at any time. Both loads of buck-shot were fired and Cook was killed instantly, his head being nearly shot off. It is doubtful if he knew who shot him, as his death was instantaneous.

Mr. James White, who was less than a half-mile from the scene of the tragedy, heard the gunshots and a few minutes later met Bohannon, who told him he had just shot "a d--n thief." Mr. White went to where Cook's body was lying, beside the railroad track, with his head in the water of a ditch. Cook was dead, and a loaded revolver was in his pocket. Willie Connell, a small boy living in the neighborhood, saw Bohannon get out of his father's cornfield, with a gun, and a few minutes later, heard the gun-shots. He ran over to the place where the killing occurred, arriving there nearly as soon as Mr. White. [. . .] The next day, fearing trouble for his prisoner, [Sheriff Montfort] took him to the soldiers' camp, where he was kept that night in safety from the gang of Ku Klux, who wanted to get hold of the man who had killed their leader.

Bohannon was indicted on a charge of murder, by the grand jury, on the first day of the term, and his trial was set for a few days later, at that term. Five days were taken up by the trial, and all during it there was a fight for legal points by Robinson, Foree and Major, for the defendant, and Phil Lee, the Commonwealth's Attorney. On the fifth day (Oct. 12th) after hearing the evidence and arguments and devoting nearly two days to a consideration of the case the jury brought in a verdict of "guilty as charged in the indictment." [. . .] The writer, who was present, remembers distinctly the appearance of the venerable looking, bearded old man, as he stood up to answer Judge Bruce. He did not seem to be the least excited and simply said: 'Judge, I have nothing to say, except there have been many lies told in this trial, and if I had not killed Addison Cook that day, he would have killed me before this.' He then sat down and Judge Bruce sentenced him "to be hanged until he is dead" on Friday, Dec. 29th, 1871. [. . .] On Dec. 23rd the higher court rendered a decision reversing the lower court and remanded the case for retrial. [. . .]

At the March term, 1872, the decision of the Court of Appeals was ordered to record, and the case of the Commonwealth vs. Bohannon was continued to the September term. At that time, upon a motion of the Commonwealth's Attorney, the case was dismissed. Mr. Bohannon lived many years, a respected and highly esteemed citizen. After the death of Addison Cook there was evidently an end to Ku Kluxism, for no more trouble came to the people of that vicinity. At the trial of several *young men charged with the assault of the negro mail agent it was demonstrated that Addison Cook, then dead, was the guilty party and nothing further was done about it.*

During the troublous times, good citizens of that vicinity suffered much by mistreatment at the hands of the Ku Klux and from threats that were made. Addison Cook, upon one occasion, ran a man by the name of "Chick" Johnson out of the town of Bagdad, threatening to kill him. His action did not meet with the approval of good citizens, and some of them did not hesitate to express their indignation at such proceedings. Among these was Mr. W. C. Baskett, a farmer who lived near Bagdad. A few days before Cook was killed, Mr. Baskett received note which read as follows:

> Headquarters K. K. K.
> General Order No. 5
> Mr. W. C. Baskett:
>
> If it appears on examination that you and "Jim" White are connected with W. C. Johnson, in any shape, manner or form, whatever, you had better prepare for leaving this country forever.
>
> Respectfully, KU KLUX KLAN
> P.S. - Contempt of this notice is death.
> Respectfully, ETC.

The death of Cook and the disorganization of the Ku Klux Klan was a great relief to many, who felt that their lives and property were in danger.

Hiram Bohannon (1846-1912), the man who shot and killed Addison Cook was the son of William (Henry?) Bohannon, Justice of the Peace of Shelby County. William was the son of John Bohannon (1755-?) and Helen Cook. Helen was the sister of **Abraham Cook** (Joshua's grandfather) and the aunt of Addison Cook's father. Helen was, then, Addison's great aunt as well as Hiram Bohannon's great grandmother. Addison was a first cousin to Joshua Flood Cook.

FROM STRENGTH TO STRENGTH

J.F. Cook's tendency to recall only what was congenial to his audience suggests how, from 1859 until his retirement in 1900, he moved from strength to strength in a respectable career. His success was dependent upon intelligence, amiability and administrative skills but also upon a cool talent for putting at their ease other stakeholders in the society in which he thrived. His call for "wise" and "most conservative" action as to relations between the races was intended to dispel any faint anxiety that Joshua, in his role as preacher and educator, might leverage his influence in the interests of some kind of dangerous racial or social reform.

The personal style Joshua discovered by his mid twenties, if not earlier, that worked well for him in his long public life, was to divide things between the abstract and the practical. In the abstract, slavery was of course wrong; but as a practical matter, the slaves, at least those in Kentucky and certainly those held by *his* family, were uniformly happy even while they were lamentably disadvantaged by their inherent low intelligence, that tragic mark upon the race of Ham. (Page 198, above.)

The interplay between abstraction and actual life was revealed to Joshua in other ways. Strong drink was a moral danger, against which he energetically worked to protect his LaGrange College students. But in the romanticized Kentucky of Joshua's youth, whiskey needed to be plentiful. In old age, Joshua recalls such events as a corn shucking or a hog-killing, when home-brew was omnipresent. On these occasions, everything was done in good fun and, any way, it was just "the negroes," those poor creatures of low intelligence, who thought Joshua's dad was drunk when he shot a pig in the face, not to kill it but to hear it squeal. Everyone laughed at his father's pranks and jests, Joshua recalled seventy years later, even if the

Joshua Flood Cook

antics involved liquor, gunfire and the maiming of slaughter animals. (For details, see **All of the Above II.**)

In fact, Joshua's idyllically-remembered boyhood home seems to have been destroyed when his father died and his mother re-married. In 1912, in the last letter he wrote - to his son, Cecil - Joshua confessed (for the first time?) that the anxieties he displayed in adolescence caused those close to him (his mother? his step-father?) to consider sending him to an asylum of some kind.

The youthful Joshua Cook, mired in the blacksmith shop for three years, was helpless to prevent the downward turn in his personal prospects. His father had died. This was an abandonment young Joshua could not repair. He could not ever again look to that source for counsel or support. My conclusion is that the death of his father caused a terror within Joshua, a terror of losing his one chance out of the smithy's shop: an education. Fear of becoming trapped in a harsh and limiting trade seems to have become the engine used by the self-confident and engaging J. F. Cook to launch himself into the wider world.

Returned from Missouri, finally in college, and apparently unwelcome in his step-father's home (or unwilling to live in it), young Joshua visited in the homes of his socially important college chums, whose fathers could help Joshua into important connections. No doubt he made the most of his Missouri connections, forged when he was a boy, living in the home of uncle Noah Flood. How else could he have been plucked from Kentucky by Missouri Baptists to operate a college?

J. F. Cook was a survivor and more than that. He was a career winner in a region devastated by enslavement, civil war, and economic and social turmoil. His memoir is testimony to his survival and (if read carefully) to how he was able to pull it off.

In 1912, knowing he was dying, Joshua wrote a loving, last letter to his youngest son, Cecil ("My precious Boy"), then 41 years old. Fortunate to have such an affectionate, affirmative statement from our ancestor, we give Joshua Flood Cook the last word.

"As a grandfather if possible I grow more affectionate. I love all my children as my own soul and D__ [wife, Drusilla] *as a part of myself body and soul. I believe man and wife are one and in everything & praying for you and yours - Blanche & Dorland as one body. I think I pray for you one hundred times or more a week. Some nights I hear the clock strike every hour and 1/2 hour for ten hours. I just lie and try to sleep but fail. I always remember you at times you preach - earnestly every Sunday...*

I have lain down & rested & I want to close this with every expression of love. I do love you and thank you for your constant love and goodness to me. God bless you and yours always. My prayers to my dying hour will be for you and should I get to heaven and if it is possible I will be praying for you there. Dear little Howard and I have a prayer service every night. - he prays sweetly "for all our dear ones" often by name - "for forgiveness of sins - to be kept from sin and that in the 'sweet by and by' we may meet on the beautiful shore" - I am doing my best to direct him heavenward - sometimes, often he closes – 'may we light in that beautiful world at last.'

Good bye
Bushels of love to all,
Daddy"

▪▪▪

SOURCES:

Joshua F. Cook, Cook family, and Susan G Framer genealogy, generally: the unpublished genealogical book by **Betty Taylor Cook** (1918-2000), mother of the writer.

Joshua Cook's career in LaGrange Missouri: see **History of Lewis, Clark, Knox and Scotland Counties, Missouri** (1887), Reprinted, Stevens Publishing Co, Astoria, Illinois 61501, pages 731-A to 732-AJ. and made available through the generosity of Farmer descendent Carolyn Farmer Wickens.

For Cook and Farmer genealogy: See Ellery Farmer, **A Farmer Book**, an essential source which has been generously posted in its entirety on the web. geocities.com/Heartland/Flats/7314/Farmer/ekam.

The present review of Joshua's life is indebted to the research conducted and generously shared by J.F. Cock's first cousin, twice removed, Charles L. Cook, of Lexington, KY. Please see ancestorstories.org. Another invaluable internet-based repository is the creation of Gary Kueber. Kueber's well documented archive can be consulted with profit. Gary, a first cousin of Joshua Cook, four times removed, has traced dozens of family lines. Please consult: kueber.us/.

he got so warm he scarcely would sit on his saddle – In 1829, William Hickman (1747-1830/34) wrote a memoir, which so described John Goode and which is appended to **All of the Above II** by this writer.

For John Murphy: Spencer's **History of Kentucky Baptists From 1769-1885** (1886, Vol I, page 387), but especially Elizabeth L Nichols, **Cook, Murphy, Hodges: Families of Early Virginia in the Ancestry of Elizabeth L Nichols** (2004, privately printed). Nichols' sources include **History of the Rev. William Murphy and his Descendants, 1798-1818** (1918), on the web at: **pastracks.com/murphy/murphytoc**

Much of the Cook material posted by Gary Kueber (see above) was created by William L Scroggins. The narrative of the killing of Addison Cook (reproduced here) has been published on line at kueber.us/, provided by Scroggins. Bill Scroggins cites as his source, **Some Old Time History of Shelbyville and Shelby County**, Ed. D. Shinnick, (columns from the *Shelby Record*, 1916-18) reprinted by Blue Grass Press, Frankfort, 1974.

For J.F. Cook's activities in Missouri: See ***The Baptist Encyclopedia*** (Philadelphia: Louis W. Everts, 1881, William Carthcart, Editor, p. 272) and **Hannibal-LaGrange College History** by J. Hurley & Roberta Hasgood, 1995, p. 130; both made available by the generosity of Charles L Cook, as specified above. See also **History of Missouri Baptists**, J. R. Douglass, Kansas City: Western Publishing Company, 1934, pages 507-09, shared by Charles L Cook. (See above Sources.) Additional biographical information: **History of Lewis, Clark, Knox and Scotland Counties, Missouri** (1887), Reprinted, Stevens Publishing Co, Astoria, Illinois 61501, pages 731-A to 732-AJ., and made available through the generosity of Farmer descendent, Carolyn Farmer Wickens.

Some biographical details concerning Susan Good Farmer Cook, may be found in a LaGrange *Democrat* obituary of her, preserved by Betty Cook and also provided generously by Farmer descendent and skilled genealogist Carolyn Farmer Wickens.

Additional J.F. Cook biographical details taken from "Dr. Joshua Flood Cook Years, 1866-1896," **Hannibal LaGrange College History**, J. Hurley and Roberta Hasgood (Marcelene, MO. Jostens: 1995, Chapter 2, made available by the generosity of Charles L Cook.

For the "Abstract of College Laws" see **Frontiers, the Story of the Missouri Baptist Convention**, J. Gordon Kingsley, Jefferson City MO: Missouri Baptist Historical Commission, 1983, page 89, available through the generosity of Charles L Cook.

INDEX

Alexander, Loveday, 167, 169, 185, 205
apocalyptic (adj), 57, 74, 166, 167, 182
Apostle Paul, 10, 53, 133, 165, 171
Aquinas, Thomas, 54, 84
Associated Farmers, see terror, 31
Aune, David, 167
Baptists, 46, 48, 49, 203, 204, 211, 213, 214
Barclay, John M.G., 169, 171, 173, 174
Barrett, C.K., 116, 118
Barth, Karl, 131, 136
Barton, Stephen, 133, 203
Bauer, W., 104, 106, 115, 118, 130
Beard, Charles A. & Mary, 42
Betz, Hans D., 59, 86, 87, 172
Bonfoeffer, Dietrich, 142
Bornkamm, G., 65, 87, 115, 118, 133
Bracero Program, 31, 32
Braceros, 32
Brown, Robert McK., 100, 118, 200

Bultmann, R., 54, 56, 59, 81, 84, 86, 114, 118
Burton, E., 54, 56, 64, 81, 84, 85, 87, 88, 133
California, 15, 23, 24, 25, 27, 29, 31, 32, 34, 35, 36, 37, 40, 41, 42, 43
Calvin, John, 53, 84
Cannery and Agricultural Workers International Union, 31
Cardozo, Benjamin, 51
Carr, E.H., 174
Carthcart, William, 214
Celts, 53, 54, 73, 78, 84, 88, 179, 180
chattel slaves, 21
Chavez, Cesar, 15, 40, 148
cheap foreign labor, 32
Chinese, 24, 25, 27, 29
Christian Jews, 53, 57, 64, 66, 82
Christians, 14, 16, 19, 38, 47, 53, 84, 96, 99, 100, 101, 104, 110, 112, 116, 117, 126, 129, 135, 168, 175

Civil War, 4, 22, 25, 163, 164, 186, 197, 198, 199, 201
Classen, Joachim, 171, 172
Cohen,, 40
Cohen, Jerry, Esq., 40
Coles, Robert, 40
collective bargaining, 14, 15, 32, 34, 35, 36, 37, 155
Committees of Vigilance, 31
Constantine, Emperor, 45
Conzelmann, Hans, 133
Cook, Betty Taylor (1918-2000), 200, 214
Cook, Cecil V Cook, Jr (1913-1970), 185, 200
Cook, Cecil V, Sr (1871-1948), 185, 200
Cook, Charles L, 213
Cook, Joshua F. Cook (1834-1912), 2, 185, 186, 187, 188, 189, 190, 191, 194, 195, 196, 197, 198, 199, 200, 201, 202, 204, 205, 208, 209, 210, 211, 212, 213, 214
Cook, Susan Goode Farmer (1838-1890), 186, 192, 193, 194, 195
Creation, 14, 16, 19, 39, 100, 143, 149, 151, 155, 213
Creator, 39
crew leader, labor contractor, 23
criminal syndicalism, 30, 31
cruel and unscrupulous, 20
Cunliffe, Marcus, 41
Daniel, Cletus, 40, 41, 42
De la Cruz, Juana Inés, 5, 140, 158
Depression (of 1893), 25
Depression, the Great (of 1929), 30, 31
Diaspora Judaism, 55
Dibelius, Martin, 114, 118, 121, 130, 133
DiGeorgio Corporation, 35
Douglass, J. R., 214
Drake, Susan Samuels, 5, 148
Dunn, J.D.G., 53, 54, 64, 75, 84, 87, 88, 90, 131, 132, 137, 175
Dunne, John G., 43
Durst, W. B, 29
East, Clay, see SFTU, 30

Elliott, Susan M., 5, 179, 180, 181, 182, 183, 184, 195
Engberg-Pedersen, Troels, 4, 165
Esler, Philip, 54, 56, 60, 81, 83, 84, 85, 86, 87, 88, 89, 91, 175
Evangelistic activity, 93, 107, 111, 123, 128
farm workers, 13, 14, 15, 16, 17, 19, 20, 23, 24, 26, 30, 31, 32, 33, 34, 35, 36, 37, 38, 42
Farmer, Ellery, 192, 213
Farmers, 30, 31
Filipinos, 27, 36
First Amendment, 3, 45, 47, 48, 49, 50
Fitzgerald, John T., 169
Fodell, Beverly, 40
Fortna, Robert, 90
Framer, Susan Goode (1838-1890), 212
Fredriksen, Paula, 90, 175
French Revolution, 47
Fung, Raymond, 116, 118
Gadamer, H.., 59
Galarza, Ernesto, 42
Galatia, 3, 53, 54, 57, 59, 62, 64, 65, 66, 70, 71, 72, 75, 80, 81, 82, 83, 84, 86, 89, 90, 92, 94, 103, 106, 108, 123, 124, 128, 134, 171, 174, 175, 176, 179, 184
Galatians, 5, 54, 55, 56, 59, 60, 61, 64, 67, 71, 77, 78, 79, 81, 83, 84, 85, 86, 87, 88, 89, 90, 91, 94, 95, 101, 106, 107, 108, 111, 124, 128, 132, 134, 137, 165, 171, 172, 173, 174, 175, 176, 179, 180, 181, 183
Garrison, William Lloyd, 22
Gaventa, Beverly, 90
Glasser, Arthur F., 114, 118
Goldfarb, Ronald L., 40
good news, 93, 96, 97, 105, 111, 122, 127
Gospel, 14, 64, 66, 77, 93, 99, 102, 105, 106, 107, 108, 109, 110, 111, 116, 121, 122, 123, 124, 125, 126, 127, 128, 131
Grondin, Jean, 86
Gruen, E.C., 55, 85
Haacker, Klaus, 133
haciendas, 23, 24
Haenchen, Ernst, 91, 133
Haight, Governor, 23

Hartmire, Wayne, 117
Hasgood, J. Hurley & Roberta, 214
Hawking, Stephen, 4, 149, 150, 151
Heidegger, Martin, 59
Heisenberg, Werner, 151
Hengle, Martin, 168
Herman, Judith L., 79, 86, 90
Home Mission Council of North America, 33
Homestead Act of 1862, 22
Hurtado, Larry, 133, 137
Immigration Exclusion Act, 25
International Workers of the World (IWW), 30
Jamaica, 32
Japanese, 27, 155, 156, 195
Jefferson, Thomas, 19, 24, 48, 49
Jensen, Joan M., 41
Jerome, Saint, 40, 53, 54, 135
Jerusalem, 58, 72, 82, 83, 87, 89, 90, 93, 97, 101, 102, 104, 111, 127, 128, 153
Jewett, Robert, 135, 175

Johnson, Luke Timothy, 137, 138, 208
Joyce, James, 4, 147
Judaea, 124
Judaism, 4, 55, 56, 58, 61, 63, 67, 68, 76, 77, 78, 80, 81, 86, 88, 104, 132, 135, 165, 167, 168
Junia, Apostle, 101, 104
Kagawa, Toyohiko, 4, 155, 156
Käsemann,, Ernst, 56, 85, 86, 91, 115, 117, 119, 121, 130, 133
Kennedy, William, 4, 145, 146
Kingsley, J. Gordon, 214
Knox, John, 87, 114, 119, 121, 130, 133, 165
Koenig, John, 114, 119
Kueber, Gary, 213
Kümmel, W.G., 114, 118, 121, 130
Kuula, Kari, 60, 61, 81, 86, 89
Lategan, B.C., 176
law (Torah), 73
Levy, Jacques, 40
Lightfoot, J.B., 53, 54, 56, 64, 84, 85, 87
Lincoln, Abraham, 163

Longenecker, Bruce, 134
Louisiana, 28, 41, 51, 204
Luther, Martin, 45, 53, 54, 84
Mack, B., 59, 60, 63, 86, 87, 91
Macquarrie, John, 86
Martin, Luther, 45
Martin, Troy, 172
Martyn, J. Louis, 53, 54, 56, 64, 81, 83, 84, 86, 87, 88, 89, 90, 91, 117, 118, 119, 131, 172, 173, 174, 175
McKinley, Wm. (President), 26, 41
McKnight, S., 55, 85
McPherson, James, 4, 163, 164
McWilliams, Cary, 41, 42
Mead, Sidney, 48, 50
Meeks, Wayne, 54, 84, 115, 119, 165, 176
Merwin, W.S., 4, 159, 160, 161
Methodists, 48
Mexican, Mexico, 27, 36
Meyer, p.w., 90
Migrant Ministries, 33, 34, 35
migrant ministry, 13, 33
missionary-organizer, 93, 96, 97, 99, 105, 109, 112, 114, 115, 121, 129
Mitchell, Margaret H., 166
Morgan, Robert, 132, 138, 139
Munck, J., 54, 81, 84, 114, 119, 121, 130
Murphy O'Connor, Jerome, 135
Murphy, John (1752-1818), 202, 203, 204, 213
Nanos, Mark, 5, 54, 56, 60, 81, 85, 86, 171, 175, 176
National Council of Churches, 33
National Farm Worker Ministry (NFWM), 37, 117
National Labor Relations Act, 30
Nichols, Elizabeth L, 203, 213
Paul the Apostle, 14, 39, 66, 85, 119, 130
Philippines, 26
Preach (Proclaim), 77, 93, 94, 96, 97, 105, 106, 107, 109, 111, 112, 121, 122, 123, 125, 126, 127, 128, 129, 203, 212

Quakers, 46
racism, 19, 38, 128, 157
Räisänen, H., 54, 61, 82, 84, 86, 87, 88, 90, 91
Reconstruction, 22, 197, 200, 204
Riesner, R., 91
Robertson, A.T., 107, 119
Roestzel, C.J., 138
Romans, 13, 14, 16, 39, 57, 61, 80, 81, 85, 90, 93, 94, 101, 102, 104, 110, 111, 128, 132, 135, 136, 137, 165
Rosner, Brian, 134
Roth, Philip, 4, 153, 154
Sanders, E.P., 61, 78, 90, 132, 137
Schildgen, Robert, 4, 155
Schoeps, H.J., 63, 86, 137
Schüssler Fiorenza, E., 115, 119, 132
Schweitzer, Albert, 56, 61, 85, 114, 119, 121, 130, 156
Schweizer, E., 167
Scroggins, William L, 213
Segal, Alan, 136
Shinnick, Ed D, 213
slavery, 9, 22, 23, 67, 163, 164, 197, 199, 200, 201, 202, 203, 209, 213
Southern Tenant Farmers Union (STFU), 30
Spain, 23, 135
Spencer, J H, 186, 203, 213
Stearns, Shubal, 202
Stowers, S., 168
strikes, 29, 31
terror, 10, 31, 62, 211
Tjerandsen, Carl, 42
Tooni, Linda Lewis, 31, 42
Torah, 10, 54, 55, 57, 58, 61, 63, 67, 68, 69, 72, 73, 74, 76, 77, 78, 81, 82, 83, 87, 88, 89, 90, 91, 137, 176, 182
Tronier, Henrik, 166, 167, 168
Tubman, Harriet, 22
United Farm Workers (UFW), 15, 37, 40
United States, 9, 10, 20, 21, 28, 34, 42, 45, 49, 50, 86, 156, 164, 203
Updike, John, 4, 143, 144
Vassilchikov, Marie, 3, 141
victims, 9, 10, 11, 19, 53, 54, 57, 58, 60, 61,

62, 63, 64, 65, 66, 67, 72, 73, 75, 76, 79, 80, 81, 82, 83, 89, 90, 92, 123, 176, 204
vigilantes, 30, 31
Vos, Johan S., 175
Walter, Nikolaus, 130, 175
Washington, George, 21, 41

Whitman, Walt, 5, 6, 7, 12, 18, 52, 120, 162, 178
Wickins, Carolyn Farmer, 213, 214
Witherington, Ben, 132
Woodward, C. Vann, 41, 164
Wrede, W., 56, 61, 85
Zinn, Howard, 42

www.ingramcontent.com/pod-product-compliance
Ingram Content Group UK Ltd.
Pitfield, Milton Keynes, MK11 3LW, UK
UKHW041430180426
11947UKWH00007B/365